MAMA'S PEARLS

By

Sylvia Villasenor

Published by Hemingway publishers
Cover design by Hemingway publishers
ISBN: Printed in the United State

CONTENTS

Dedication v

Acknowledgment vii

About the Author ix

Introduction... xi

Chapter 1 The Author's Beginning...2

Chapter 2 Key Characters 22

Chapter 3 Setting the Stage..44

Chapter 4 Trials and Tribulations 74

Chapter 5 Moments of Connection 98

Chapter 6 Reflecting on Growth 116

Chapter 7 Love As a Guiding Force 132

Chapter 8 Strength in Adversity 144

Chapter 9 Passing on the Pearls..158

Conclusion 168

Dedication

To my mother, a guiding star I never truly met but have always felt beside me.

Through the stories of those who loved you, I found pieces of your spirit—strength, resilience, and a love that knows no bounds. This book is for you, my beacon of inspiration, and my heart's everlasting compass. You have shaped me in ways words cannot fully capture, and this story, born from our family's journey, is my way of honoring you.

Acknowledgment

Writing this memoir has been a journey through memories, both sweet and bittersweet, and I am deeply grateful to those who have been a part of my story.

To my family, whose unwavering support and love have been my foundation—each of you has played an essential role in shaping who I am. My siblings, who shouldered burdens and celebrated joys alongside me, have been my strength and my guiding lights. Through trials and triumphs, we have stood together, and I am forever grateful for the bond we share.

To my friends and loved ones, thank you for believing in me, for listening to my stories, and for encouraging me to tell them. Your support has been invaluable in this journey.

To those who opened their hearts and shared their memories, stories, and wisdom—thank you. Your insights helped bring depth to these pages and brought a fuller understanding of our family's history.

Lastly, to my readers, thank you for joining me in this journey through past generations and family legacies. May this book serve as a reminder of the resilience found within family bonds and the strength that can be drawn from our roots.

About the Author

Sylvia Villasenor was born in Los Angeles, CA. She is the daughter of immigrants that moved to the U.S. from Mexico in the mid 1950's. In 1985 she obtained a Bachelor of Science and a Real Estate license and worked as a mortgage loan officer for thirty years. She married her college sweetheart in 1988 and together they raised three children. Now she is retired and has written two momoirs and a children's book about growing up in mid Los Angeles with her widowed father and six siblings in which she describes in detail the challenges the family had as first and second immigration family living in Los Angeles give her the encouragement and resilience to overcome the obstacles to obtain the life her father dream of for his family.

Introduction

The weight of the world often rests on a single pair of shoulders. In my story, my father carried it. His back, a roadmap of toil, bore the scars of a journey that spanned continents and cultures. He carried not just his own dreams but the hopes of an entire family. His story is a testament to the enduring human spirit, a blueprint for survival etched into the heart of the American Dream.

This memoir tells the true story of my father and his children, capturing the essence of a typical immigrant family and aiming to resonate with people worldwide. The United States, a land built by immigrants, has always been a beacon for those seeking a better life. Long before any of us arrived, the indigenous people were the original inhabitants. Over time, this country has welcomed the brave souls who come first to pave the way for themselves and their families. My father was one such brave soul.

He arrived here with dreams of a better life, making countless sacrifices for us, his children. As the youngest of seven, I felt compelled to write about what happened to him, perhaps to understand my roots and honor the strength and courage he embodied. This story is not just about him but also about how his journey shaped us and how we continue to carry his torch.

When we first moved here, we were just kids, unaware of the sacrifices he and my mother made. We lived one day at a time, oblivious to the challenges that lay ahead. It was only as we grew older that we began to see the opportunities he created for us. Doors slowly began to open; we just had to walk in and learn the trade. These opportunities in the 1960's were unimaginable back in Mexico, where women got married young, stayed home, and had children. Regardless of whether their husbands turned out good or bad, they stuck it out. My dad didn't want that for us. He saw how women suffered in small towns, sometimes moving back in with their parents, crammed into one room with four or five kids. "No, no, no," he said, "I don't want that for my children."

Even though his heart was hardened by his own troubles, now that I'm grown, I can feel his pain. He carried the weight of our future on his shoulders, determined to provide us with a life of opportunity and freedom. His sacrifices laid the foundation for our success, and his unwavering resolve taught us the value of perseverance.

Mom must have been a headstrong individual because our maternal grandmother told my older sisters stories about her indomitable spirit, her strength, and how she faced every challenge with courage. They could see a spark in her eyes whenever she talked about mom, a thunderbolt of pride for her daughter. I wonder if my mother looked just like her mother. I can picture my mom, sketching her in my mind with every detail that my grandmother shared about her. This description of her personality is engraved in my mind, and I hold on to it like a precious painting.

It does fill a void in my heart that she didn't live longer, so I could have created some memories with her to cherish after her departure.

All I have are stories of her strength, sacrifices, and compromises that she made—being with my father, getting married at a very young age, and bearing seven children.

I remember my father's weary eyes, often filled with a mixture of exhaustion and unwavering determination. His laughter, though rare, was a cherished sound, a momentary glimpse of the joy he kept hidden beneath the weight of his burdens. My father was a good man, but his time wasn't good.

My siblings, each a pillar of support, played their part in shaping the person I would become. Their struggles and triumphs were woven into the fabric of our family, each thread a testament to our collective resilience. My brother's protective nature, my sisters' nurturing spirits, and the unspoken bond we shared created a sanctuary of love and understanding. Every glance, every word, and every moment spent together became a pearl of wisdom, guiding me through the labyrinth of life.

Through this memoir, I hope to inspire first-generation immigrants and remind later generations of their heritage. By sharing our family's journey, I aim to foster empathy and compassion for those who are just beginning their voyage. This is a story of love, loss, the unbreakable bond of family, and hardships to achieve one's goals; meant to inspire and remind us all of the power of dreams and the sacrifices made to achieve them. Each page is a tribute to the enduring spirit of immigrants, a chronicle of our struggles and triumphs, and a celebration of the legacy we build for future generations. May this memoir serve as a beacon of hope and a reminder that the American Dream is a tapestry woven with the threads of countless stories like ours.

The book unfolds in three distinctive sections, each revealing different facets of our story and the lessons learned along the way. The first section, "The Foundations," delves into the foundational aspects of our family's history, exploring our early beginnings, the influential characters who shaped our lives, and the environments that shaped our upbringing and initial life lessons.

In the second section, "The Emotional Tapestry," I delve deeper into the emotional aspects of our journey. Here, I recount the trials and tribulations we faced as a family, including the emotional struggles and significant moments of connection that strengthened our bonds. Reflecting on our growth, both individually and as a family, reveals profound realizations that emerged from overcoming our challenges.

The final section, "Pearls of Wisdom," distills the core messages of love, strength, and courage that define our family's experience. It shares stories of how love guided our decisions, instances where determination proved crucial, and insights into passing on these pearls of wisdom to future generations. Each section offers practical and inspirational takeaways, encouraging readers to apply these lessons in their own lives.

I have compiled this book in nine chapters. Each section offers an in-depth look into the early days of our lives as immigrants, to overcoming struggles with diligence and hope for a brighter tomorrow. In the introduction, you'll get a sense of why I wrote this book and the significance of "Mama's Pearls." I'll share my heart and soul with you, offering a glimpse into the journey we're about to take together. You'll see how themes of love, strength, and valor weave through my story, setting the stage for the chapters ahead.

The first chapter, "The Author's Beginning," is focused on the details of the characters you'll meet in this book, understanding my life and the key figures who have shaped my voyage. In the second chapter, "Key Characters," I'll take you back to my early life. You'll learn about my family background, my childhood experiences, and the significant role my mother played in shaping my values and outlook on life. The third chapter, "Setting the Stage," will teleport you to the challenges of immigrant life and the cultural dynamics of my community. You'll get a vivid picture of the world I grew up in.

The fourth chapter, "Trials and Tribulations," explains the emotional struggles and difficult times we endured, offering a raw and honest portrayal of my fortitude. In the fifth chapter, "Moments of Connection," I'll highlight significant moments of bonding and understanding between my mother and my father, as well as challenging moments due to his anger and desperation as a single widowed father of seven children. The sixth chapter, "Reflecting on Growth," offers a picture of growth and discovery, reflecting on the transformative power of resolve and the lessons I learned through life's harsh challenges.

Chapter five, "Love as a Guiding Force," offers practical and inspirational takeaways for my readers enriched by my personal experiences of family strength, love, hardships, and never giving up.

In the eighth chapter, "Strength in Adversity," you'll uncover instances where strength and persistence were crucial and the only options available. Through some tough times and figuring out how to get by, my life shows just how strong we can be when we need to. In the final chapter, "Passing on the Pearls," I'll talk about why it's so important to share what we've learned and help others grow. There's some practical advice on how to pass down these lessons to future generations so the legacy of love and staying headstrong in love keeps going.

Being the youngest of seven, with five older sisters and one brother, I learned a lot from my siblings' experiences—what to do and what not to do. I closely observed their choices, seeing what worked for them and what didn't. Though I made my own mistakes along the way, I always knew we were better off here in the United States than in our country of origin. While we deeply love and admire our mother country, my dad had a clear vision for us: better opportunities, better education, and the chance for all of us, especially women, to be self-sufficient. He wanted us to have the ability to support ourselves and our families, regardless of our circumstances.

I worked hard to achieve the goals my dad set for us. Despite the challenges and hardships we faced, my father remained steadfast in his belief that America offered us a chance at a brighter future. His determination and sacrifices, despite the difficulties he encountered, were always rooted in his desire to provide the best for his children.

Being the youngest child of seven, I never really knew my mom because she passed away when I was just four months old. Despite this tremendous loss, we were fortunate in ways many others are not. Close family members stepped in, taking us into their homes and helping my dad raise us. My father provided a solid foundation for how we should live our lives, emphasizing working toward our faith. Yes, he believed that if you work smartly and stay determined, you can actually change your own future.

Raised Catholic, we stayed close to the Church, grounding our lives in Christian values. Our lives took a significant turn when we left those supportive family members and returned to the States to live with my father. That's when the real challenges began. Suddenly, we were seven kids with a single father struggling to make ends meet. His frustration was palpable, especially when he lost his job. My older siblings, the eldest just seventeen, had to step up. They started working while continuing their education, trying to help keep our family afloat.

As a young child, I absorbed all this. At eight years old, I felt their pain and tension. It was a time when my childhood was overshadowed by the weight of our struggles. Playing outside was an escape, but coming back home meant facing the harsh realities. I often wondered how I could help, but all I could do was take things one day at a time, watching my sisters leave home at young ages, thinking they might find a better life by marrying young, even falling in love, and starting their own families.

However, their early marriages often led to difficult times. By the age of nine or ten, I already knew I didn't want that life for myself. I wanted something better. I wanted to stay in school to prepare myself so that if I ever faced the same struggles as my dad, I would be ready to stand on my own. Observing my sisters, I saw not only their hardships but also their incredible strength. They faced their challenges head-on, becoming the pillars of their households.

One of my sisters endured a tumultuous marriage with a young, rebellious husband who struggled with unemployment and depression. Despite this, she worked tirelessly at Pacific Bell, eventually becoming a successful salesperson and providing a good life for her children. She never gave up on her husband, supporting him until he eventually recovered. Her resilience was a testament to the strength our father had instilled in us.

Another sister went through a divorce and raised her two children alone. She faced the terrifying ordeal of her child battling cancer, but she never wavered, dedicating herself to supporting her family and helping others. She became a lifeline for Hispanic families at the Children's Hospital, helping them navigate the complex healthcare system and secure financial aid. Even now, retired, she continues to help those in need, assisting immigrants from other countries. Seeing these strong women in my life inspired me and showed me that I, too, could overcome any obstacles. Their determination and support bolstered my dreams, assuring me that I would be okay no matter what life threw my way.

This memoir is not just a story of my family's struggles and triumphs; it's a tribute to the resilience and love that defined our lives. Through the lessons of "Mama's Pearls," I hope to inspire others who face similar challenges, offering a message of hope, strength, and the enduring power of family.

I often find myself thinking about my grandchildren, the joy they bring to my life, and how different it feels from when I was raising my own children. Back then, I wasn't always around. Work demanded my time, and I couldn't be the mother I wanted to be at every moment. Now, with my grandchildren, I have the chance to savor the moments I missed with my kids. But more than that, I want to leave behind a written legacy for them—something tangible that tells the story of our family, reaching back through the generations.

When I reflect on my life, I realize how little we often know about the lives of our grandparents. We know them, yet the details of their journeys remain hidden, their stories untold. Imagine if you had a book written by your grandmother, filled with the experiences and lessons she learned. This memoir is my gift to my grandchildren and their children—a way for them to truly know where they come from and the journey that has shaped our family.

As I paint the canvas with our story, offering intricate details, I hope to inspire others—both immigrants navigating their own journeys and those born here—to appreciate the sacrifices made by so many to build a better life and to foster empathy and understanding across communities.

"Mama's Pearls" is a heartfelt memoir that chronicles the journey of my father and our family as immigrants in the United States. It's a story that resonates with the experiences of many who have sought a better life in a new land. My father's decision to leave his homeland was driven by dreams of opportunities and a brighter future for his children. As the youngest witness of all the hardships time threw at us, I've long felt compelled to document my family's courageous journey and the profound impact it had on our lives.

Throughout the narrative, "Mama's Pearls" symbolizes the wisdom and values passed down by my mother's, guidance through the challenges of our immigrant experience. These pearls encapsulate invaluable life lessons that shaped our resilience and unity as a family. They are a testament to the enduring influence of my father, who played a pivotal role in nurturing and supporting us through our journey.

Chapter 1
The Author's Beginning

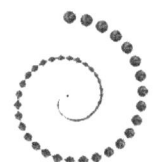

Can you imagine the ache of a child growing up without her mother? My mother passed away when I was very young, leaving behind a void that has never quite been filled. Her absence is a constant ache in my heart, a lingering reminder of motherly love and guidance I lost too soon and one I really never knew. Despite this emptiness, her spirit lives on in the stories my maternal grandmother and Nina Jose, mom's sister, shared with us, painting a vivid picture of a woman whose life was a beautiful tapestry of courage, love, and selfless sacrifice.

My mother was the oldest of her siblings, and in many ways, she was like a second mother to them. From a young age, she stepped up to help her own mother, taking care of her younger brothers with a kindness and sense of responsibility that belied her years. She was the one who would soothe a crying child, bandage a scraped knee, and offer a comforting embrace in times of distress. Her nurturing nature was a beacon of warmth and stability in a household often shadowed by hardship.

Growing up in a small suburban town, my mother's opportunities for education were limited by the rigid orthodox taboos of the time. In her era, girls were rarely encouraged to pursue schooling beyond the sixth grade. Secondary and high school education was seen as unnecessary and often impractical, as it meant traveling to the city or moving to another state. For most families, this was not an option. Yet, despite these barriers, my mother excelled in her studies up to the point she was allowed. She learned to read and write remarkably well, a testament to her intelligence and determination.

Her early years were a constant balancing act between her duties at home and her desire to learn. She would often stay up late into the night, poring over her schoolbooks by the dim light of an oil lamp long after her siblings had fallen asleep. Her thirst for knowledge was insatiable, and she took great pride in her ability to read and write. To her, these skills were not just academic achievements; they were a lifeline, a connection to a world beyond the confines of her small town.

As she grew older, the pressures of societal expectations weighed heavily on her. Early marriage was a common fate for girls in her community, and my mother was no exception. She faced these challenges with the same strength and grace that had defined her from childhood. Even as she navigated the complexities of adult life, she remained a pillar of support for her family, always ready to lend a helping hand or a listening ear.

In many ways, my mother's life was a series of sacrifices. She put her dreams on hold to care for her family, uphold traditions, and fulfill the roles expected of her. Yet, in every story my grandmother told, there was a thread of quiet defiance, a sense that my mother never truly gave up on her aspirations. She found ways to educate herself, to grow, and to inspire those around her despite the constraints placed upon her.

In the era my mother lived through, early marriages for women were a common and often expected practice, driven by a complex web of social and cultural factors. Orthodox norms and traditional customs dictated that young women marry at a young age, a reflection of deeply rooted societal pressures and patriarchal values. These early unions were not just a matter of personal choice but were influenced by the limited opportunities available to women and the economic necessities of the time.

However, in the small town where my mother lived, life was a blend of hard work and family duties, and my mother was at the center of it all. As soon as she and her peers were old enough, they took on jobs at the factory—the plant, as everyone called it. These jobs were more than just work; they were lifelines, offering stability and the promise of continuity since they could be passed down to siblings or children. My mother, always diligent, balanced her plant job with mornings dedicated to our family business, working from six to ten. Can you imagine the sheer determination it took to juggle these roles? Her connections with neighbors and friends were strong, built through shared work and mutual support. Those morning hours were not just about business; they were about community and the bonds that tied everyone together.

When my mother married at twenty, she stepped into the role of wife and mother with the same dedication she brought to her work. In our town, a woman's path was clear: marry young, start a family, and devote yourself to your home. Being unmarried at twenty-one was almost scandalous, a sign of being an "old maid." But my mother embraced her domestic duties wholeheartedly. From what my older siblings tell me, she was a fantastic mom, her love and care evident in everything she did. She followed my father's guidance, ensuring our family navigated life's challenges with unity and strength. How did she manage to balance so much, to give so much of herself every day? My father wasn't perfect, but he always did his best to take care of our family. In Mexico, he worked tirelessly to provide for us, but the opportunities were limited, and he knew he couldn't offer us the life he dreamed of. Moving to the States was his way of giving us a chance at something better, even though it meant starting over in a foreign land. He worked even harder once we arrived, driven by the need to ensure our future was brighter than the past he left behind. His sacrifices and determination were fueled by love and hope, even when the odds seemed stacked against us.

I was only four months old when I lost my mother. I can't connect with her in the way most people can with their mothers because, for me, she was never there. I never remember having her by my side. I never felt her comforting presence or heard her soothing voice after that. The void she left was vast, a chasm in my young heart. After her passing, we were sent to Mexico, where my aunt, Nina Jose, became the closest thing to a mother I had. She stepped into the breach with fierce love and an unwavering dedication to our well-being.

My aunt, Nina Jose, and my maternal grandmother, who we lived with until her passing when I was five, became our pillars of strength. Yet, it was Nina Jose who truly filled the maternal role. She was a whirlwind of activity, always busy ensuring we were safe and that nothing and no one could harm us. Her love was a shield, her presence a fortress. But even in her busyness, she made sure we connected with the community around us. She encouraged us to befriend the neighbors and their children, creating a semblance of normalcy in a life that had been uprooted and changed forever. My Nina Jose might have been different from the mother I never knew, possibly more guarded and protective, but through her, I felt the closest connection to the woman who gave me life. Her efforts to shield us and her openness to the world around us were her ways of loving us, of trying to fill the gaping hole left by my mother's absence.

As a child I had two dreams about my mother, and those dreams feel as real as the air I breathe. They brought me closer to her, a woman I cannot remember. In these dreams, I find myself at a beautiful Spanish-style hacienda, its white walls gleaming under the sun and a fountain bubbling serenely outside. The setting is always the same, like a scene frozen in time. I sit by the fountain, waiting with my sisters, our hearts pounding with anticipation. When my mother finally emerges, my sisters rush to her, hugging and kissing her with the fervor of long-lost love. But I stand back, hiding behind their skirts, feeling a mix of fear and shyness. They urge me to hug her, to embrace the woman who gave me life, but I can't move. She sees my hesitation and tells them to leave me, be her voice soothing and kind. It's okay, she says, and in that moment, I feel a connection, fragile yet profound.

In another dream, we return to the same hacienda. The fountain still sings its gentle song, and we wait once more. This time, my mother bursts out of the house with rollers in her hair, her face alight with surprise. "What are you doing here?" she asks, a hint of laughter in her voice. My sister explains that we came to see her, and she smiles, though her eyes reveal a rush. "We can't stay long," she says, "I'm getting ready for a dinner party." We stay a little while, savoring the brief moments we have with her before we must leave. These dreams are so vivid they linger in my mind long after I wake. Once, I even felt like someone picked me up from my bed, carrying me on a carpet ride through scenes that flashed by too fast to grasp. I was scared, and in an instant, I was back in my bed. Was it her? I like to think it was. In those dreams and fleeting moments, I find the connection I've always longed for, a bridge to the mother I never truly knew.

I believe that the first time she appeared in my dream, it was her way of letting me know that she was still there, watching over me. In the dream, she seemed to say she missed me and that she wished she could be with us. She hovered above my head, and as she left, she kissed my forehead. I wasn't scared in the dream, but when I woke up, I felt a mixture of awe and sadness. It was as if she was reaching out from beyond, trying to bridge the gap between us. But how could I, a child who never really knew her mother, begin to connect with this ethereal presence? What do you say to someone you don't know; someone you can't remember ever being close to? The feeling of wanting to reach out but not knowing how left me unsettled.

I told my sisters about the dream, and they asked what she was wearing. I described her as looking like she did in the picture taken when she was seventeen, youthful and vibrant. It wasn't the image of her at thirty-three, worn by life and seven children, her body no longer in the best of shape. Women of her time didn't have the luxury of self-care unless they were wealthy. That dream was the closest I felt to her, aside from the stories my sisters told. Some were happy and filled with laughter and love, while others were tinged with sadness and pain. Those stories often left me feeling emotional and upset with my father, hearing how he wasn't always kind to her. The dreams and stories intertwined, painting a complex picture of a woman who, despite the hardships, remained a beacon of love and strength in my fragmented memories.

Looking back, I wonder if my father's behavior stemmed from the toll their marriage took over time. He once told me, after I got married, that after having seven kids, the passion in a marriage fades. Perhaps he had simply lost interest in her but still respected her as the mother of his children. It was clear he felt a duty to stay with her and provide for the family. But maybe, just maybe, he sought comfort elsewhere, finding solace in the company of other women. It's a painful possibility to consider, but it seems all too plausible. The complexities of their relationship and the strain of raising a large family might have created an emotional chasm that neither could bridge. My father's nights spent away, the secret meetings, and the occasional violence all point to a deeper unrest. Yet, amidst all this turmoil, he remained in the marriage, a stark reminder of the tangled web of duty and desire. This fractured reality, where love and obligation intersected with cheating and frustration, has left me with an unresolved ache, a question mark hanging over a past I can only partially understand.

It's easier for a man to disconnect and find solace elsewhere, especially someone like my father. He was a good-looking man, and his work in nightclubs exposed him to many women. In that field, it wasn't hard to imagine him having external relationships. I remember hearing stories about how my mother would sometimes meet Dad at the room downtown he rented to spend the night after his late nights at the night club he worked as a musician. She wanted to spend a little time with him; she brought him breakfast after a long night. On one such morning, she found him with another woman. Enraged, she grabbed the pot of breakfast and hurled it at the woman, sparking a physical confrontation. They wrestled, and the woman, equally furious, fought back. She managed to get hold of the now-empty pot and had my mother pinned down, ready to strike her with it. My father stepped in at the last moment, stopping the woman and reminding her, "She's the mother of my children."

SYLVIA VILLASENOR

This story passed down through the family, paints a vivid picture of the tumultuous relationship my parents had. My father might have strayed, but at that moment, he still acknowledged my mother's place in our family. It's a heartbreaking tale that adds layers to my understanding of their lives together. It reveals the raw emotions and complex dynamics that shaped our family history, and it makes me ponder the many facets of love, loyalty, and betrayal they experienced.

After that incident, my mother reached her breaking point. She couldn't endure the turmoil any longer and decided she had to leave. His mother, naturally siding with her, intervened on her behalf. She insisted that my father had to abandon the music business, which by then was no longer lucrative. She urged him to find a new path and reconnect with his younger brother, Jesse, who lived in Los Angeles. That was the turning point that led my father to let go of his musical career at the age of 38. He was ten years older than my mother, and by that stage, the choices were clear: continue with the music and remain single or adapt to a new way of life if he was committed to a family.

So, with a heavy heart and a sense of inevitability, he chose to make the change. The move to Los Angeles marked a new chapter. The unraveling of his relationships paints a picture of a man struggling to reconcile his past with his present, a man caught between the remnants of old dreams and the harsh realities of a life that demanded adaptation.

MAMA'S PEARLS

My father passed away in 2001 at the age of 86. By then, he had long been a distant figure in my life. He was not approachable or particularly close to me. His bond was stronger with my older sisters, who had spent more time with him during their formative years. They say that the first five years of a child's life are crucial for building deep connections, and by the time I left at just five months old, that window had closed for us. My father's mother, along with my mother's mother, were the ones who raised me. They filled the void left by my parents, and the closest bond I formed was with his mother, who took on a nurturing role.

My sisters, who grew up under his watchful eye, respected him deeply but were also afraid of him. The complex mixture of fear and reverence they felt was something I observed from a distance. I carried a simmering anger towards him, fueled by the stories and the way he was spoken of. I waited for the day when I would be old enough to confront him, to argue without fear and voice the frustrations I had quietly harbored.

Because of his harsh and distant nature, my older sisters didn't exactly look up to him in the way one might expect. They knew they had to follow his rules and do as he wanted because they saw the weight of his responsibilities and respected him for that. In our Mexican upbringing, respect for parents was non-negotiable and deeply ingrained from a young age. It wasn't just a matter of personal choice; it was a cultural imperative reinforced by everyone around us.

SYLVIA VILLASENOR

Times have changed dramatically. The newer generations, including my own children, have grown up differently. As church attendance dwindled and many distanced themselves from the Catholic Church, rebellion became more prevalent. It's striking how events at the church, once bustling with activity, now seem empty unless there's a funeral or major celebration. This shift away from traditional values and religious practices has led to a new kind of defiance, with children growing up in a vastly different environment from the one we knew. While we were taught to honor our elders—our parents, grandparents, aunts, and uncles—today's youth navigate a world where that respect is no longer as uniformly expected. The evolving attitudes reflect a broader cultural shift, one where the lessons of the past clash with the realities of the present.

My sisters accepted their roles with a resigned respect, but I, on the other hand, was fiercely rebellious. As a child, I couldn't comprehend the underlying reasons for his behavior, only the fear and injustice it evoked. Now, with the benefit of hindsight, I understand that his harshness stemmed from his own struggles and needs, but back then, all I saw was the looming threat of his anger. There were times when his yelling would so terrify me that I'd end up wetting my pants, a reaction to the sheer fear he instilled in me. How could I ever feel close to someone who frightened me so profoundly?

The dinner table was the worst of it all. It was where he vented his frustrations, laying them out on anyone within earshot. Our family dinners, meant to be moments of togetherness, became a battleground where his discontent was thrown at us. We were forced to endure these gatherings, feeling the weight of his anger and resentment. It was the hardest part of the day, a relentless reminder of the emotional distance between us and the father, who should have been a source of comfort, not fear.

My heart is full of so many heart-wrenching memories. Oh, some of them crush my heart into tiny pieces! I recall it was Christmas of 1965, our first holiday season since arriving in January of that year. Espe had gone back to Mexico to marry her husband over the Christmas holidays. My dad wasn't working at the time; he had lost his job during the summer, and although he might have been receiving some unemployment benefits, I prefer to think of it as if he was.

Jeannie, the oldest, was there helping out; she had managed to land a part-time job while still in high school, thanks to her honesty with our family's situation. The job provided her with clothes for school and for the office where she worked, which helped ease the burden on my father until he finally found work about six months later. During that Christmas, with Espe away in Mexico, we all sat around the table, a mix of anticipation and apprehension in the air. Tony and Sheila were whispering, trying to muster the courage to ask if we would get Christmas gifts. I was the one who finally broke the silence, asking directly, "Are we getting Christmas gifts? Is Santa Claus coming to visit?" His reaction was explosive and immediate—he shouted a firm "No," crushing the fragile hope that we might have a joyful holiday.

SYLVIA VILLASENOR

Looking back, I still feel the sting of his harsh words, "There's no Santa Claus. You guys are old enough to know," a brutal truth delivered without a trace of empathy to my six-year-old self, Lupe at seven, Tony at ten, and Sheila at eleven. His inability to offer a comforting explanation only deepened the hurt, leaving us with a raw, unspoken longing for the magic of Christmas that he had so cruelly extinguished.

As we sat around the table, the air thick with unspoken sorrow, each of us struggled to swallow our food, our throats tight with the weight of disappointment. My embarrassment and anger simmered beneath the surface as we, the youngest, hoped for some compassion, but instead, his frustration only grew. Jeanne and Ruth, unsure of how to soothe the tense atmosphere, bowed their heads in quiet resignation. Amidst this, he grudgingly mentioned that we would attend Midnight Mass on the 24th, a small promise of solace in the form of a hearty meal provided by Jeannie and Ruth, a fleeting glimmer of warmth in an otherwise bleak Christmas.

Our Christmas tree was pretty sad—a tiny, old metallic one from my uncle's stash, with some old gummies as the only decorations. It was nothing like the shiny, wrapped gifts you see on TV. Back in Mexico, Christmas meant putting our shoes outside for gifts that weren't wrapped, but this year was different. We didn't have much of anything except that pitiful tree. Thankfully, a neighbor who had become like family—because his daughter was my friend—bought gifts for Sheila, Tony, Lupe, and me. It was such a relief to get something, and we were really thankful for his kindness. That

Christmas was one of the reasons we learned to keep our mouths shut during dinner, trying to avoid adding to his stress. He took out his frustrations on the older girls and everyone else, though he was somewhat kinder to them because he knew they were trying. Back then, as a child, I didn't understand his desperation. Now that I'm older, I can't help but think, *What if that had happened to me?* It's a sobering thought, especially knowing there were nonprofit organizations or church programs that could have helped with toys for us kids. If only he had known about them. He would have asked for something for his kids if he'd known about those options, but he either didn't know or didn't want to ask for help. I was just confused by it all. That's just how he was—proud and stoic. We dealt with it, and it never happened again. But that experience taught me a valuable lesson: if I ever see someone in need, I'll step up and help.

As the years went by, we grew more resilient. The following year brought improvement. Espe's husband came to stay with us and went to school to learn English so he could fill out his own job applications. Eventually, my dad and Jaime landed jobs where Uncle Jesse worked, at Phelps Dodge. I believe it's still around in Chicago, where its main plant is located. They worked at the branch that was located in East Los Angeles. My dad and Jaime both secured permanent positions, and we even got health insurance. Meanwhile, Espe worked part-time at a company owned by a Jewish family that manufactured men's trousers. With Espe selling food on the side, our income improved. The girls were doing well, too. After Jeannie graduated from high school, she landed a job with a soap factory located near downtown L.A.

SYLVIA VILLASENOR

The following Christmas in 1967 was really special, a perfect turnaround from the previous one. We were slowly able to leave those tough times behind us.

When dad was finally able to buy his first car while living on Kenmore Ave, our weekends became fun, spending them at Griffith Park or the beach. We'd all pile into the station wagon, and he'd take us to meet Uncle Jesse and his kids for a fun picnic. We'd play outside and enjoy those simple, joyful moments. Dad was in a good mood, and he seemed happier.

We had this amazing neighbor, Katie, who became like family. She lived just four doors down and was the one who motivated Dad to buy a car. She had a station wagon, and on Friday nights, she'd take us to the drive-in. We'd all pile into the back with no seatbelts and watch Spanish movies since our English wasn't great yet. Katie knew my dad was looking for a car, so she mentioned that a station wagon like hers was up for sale and suggested he might be interested. Dad ended up buying the station wagon, and on the weekends, he and my older sisters would plan the picnics at Griffith Park or Santa Monica Beach if the weather was warm. There were weekends when Dad invited family and friends from our hometown in Mexico over for a barbeque, and he would pick them up because they didn't own a car. It felt like he was changing, not so angry anymore. But he was never one for hugs or much physical affection. I remember talking to Jeannie when I was older, and she mentioned how Dad never hugged them or got close. I told her, "He just hated us." She said, "No, no, he wasn't like that. We were six girls, and he was just the man of the house. He didn't want anyone to think he was doing anything inappropriate or that he was too close to us. He was so careful about his image." I couldn't believe it. I asked, "So we suffered from his lack of affection because of that? I mean, my mom's brother was always hugging us and showing affection." He only had one son. On my mom's side, we had just that one cousin, but he felt like a brother to us. When we lived in Mexico, his family lived in the house behind my grandma's, connected by a door to our place. He was playful and fun, generous with hugs, and easily showed warm affection. That small bit of love from him made such a difference, giving us the confidence that we were truly loved, something we missed from our dad.

Amid the constant struggle, we felt like a burden, so when I was just 14, I began searching for a job, pretending to be 16, which is the required age for a teenager to obtain a job with a work permit from the local High School. My sister Lupe worked at our local High School work permit office and easily provided me with one. I started working to buy myself some clothes because our dad was stretched thin, providing for all six of us. The older siblings pitched in, buying us what they could, but it was never enough, and we had to make everything last.

His demeanor was clear: keep your distance, don't ask questions. If he spoke to you, you responded. If he was in a good mood, he might offer a smile or a brief conversation. But his warmth was reserved for adults and his friends, who adored him. For us kids, it was like testing the waters—if they were cold, you stayed away; if they were warm, you dared to approach. We learned early on to navigate his moods and adapt accordingly.

As I grew older and had my own children, I began to understand the depth of unconditional love. There were moments when it was hard, and I would cry, wishing Mom was still alive.

During my adolescent years, I would hurt so much, crying myself to sleep. I would whisper under my blankets, crying out to mom, "I'm ready to go with you. Can you come get me?"—yearning to go home to heaven and be with my mother. Even though I knew it wasn't going to happen, those dreams of her brought comfort. The ache for my mother was a constant companion, a reminder of the love and comfort I missed out on due to her sudden death. Even though I knew I wasn't going to meet her in this life no matter how much I wanted, those dreams of her brought a bittersweet solace, allowing me to feel her embrace once more, even if only in my sleep.

God had plans for me. But I would say, "I can't take this anymore. Can you come to get me, Mom?" You know what I mean? Sometimes, things got really rough when my siblings moved out, and it was just my dad and me. Mom was the one I really connected with in spirit. Emotionally, I would connect with my paternal grandma through letters; she was still alive. My grandma passed away when I was 20. I think everybody was gone when I was 16. My brother had moved out, and Lupe left to get married at 17, around Christmas. So, it was just me and my dad. He was kinder towards me, and financially it was easier for him. As soon as we started working, we had to give him a part of your pay, which made me responsible in a sense.

As I got older, I would connect with my mother when I was feeling down. I would feel her presence, and a warmth feeling would come upon my chest. This feeling lingered on until morning, right before I left for school. Busy days at school, friends, and my part-time job helped me get through the day. Once home, I had dinner and homework to do, and by then, I was too tired and would quickly fall into a deep sleep. During my High School years Dad worked the afternoon shift, so I didn't see him much during the week since he got home around midnight. When we were younger, he worked the night shift, so we did see him during the afternoon. We had dinner with him, and he hung around until 10:00 p.m. when he left for work.

As I got older, I began to notice that he was always there for everyone, especially for us girls on each of our wedding days. Dad was always at the Church, ready to walk us down the aisle to give us away to our spouses. When I got married at 29, Dad said to me joking, "Thank God you're finally getting married. I am done." As an adult, it was easier to connect with him.

In my early twenties, while still attending the University, I left the Catholic Church to join a non-denominational Christian church led by a Jewish pastor who believed in Jesus. It was a revelation— 45 minutes of a sermon instead of the 15-20 minutes I was used to at the Catholic Church, where I often lost focus. Those were the years when you either became reckless or kept it straight, especially as I approached legal adulthood at 21. Attending this church on Sundays felt like getting reacquainted with Jesus through the passionate teachings of this Jewish pastor. I was in awe because I'd never seen anything like it before. I even prayed to marry a Jew, and it happened—though I later realized they aren't any different from us.

Dad retired and moved to Guadalajara. I didn't miss him much when he moved away. He came to visit at least three times per year, but I wasn't that excited to see him. Perhaps the lack of bonding with him during my younger years caused this cold, distant heartship between us. As I got older, I started to think that I might have been just as harsh as him if I had faced the same challenges. I began to forgive him and asked God to forgive me for harboring those feelings. When I reached the age of marriage and finally got married, I began to understand and empathize with all the emotions my parents had gone through. It was like a veil was lifted, and I could see their struggles and sacrifices with a newfound clarity. I connected deeply with my mother, especially because of the stories my grandmother and others shared about her. Those stories painted a vivid picture of her strength and love, making me feel incredibly close to her. When I was a child, I had those two clear, vivid dreams about her. Makes me believe that our connection transcends time and space. I haven't had those dreams since then, but I still remember them vividly. It was always the same house, a beautiful Spanish-style ranch, almost like she was still living there. They say what is down here is a replica of what is up there, only more alive and happier. I believe that because in my dreams, her house was so real, like a glimpse into another world. I had two dreams about that same place, and it left an impression on me. It felt like a message, a connection to her that goes beyond this life.

As I reflect on these dreams and the stories that keep my mother alive in my heart, I realize how much they have shaped my understanding of love, resilience, and connection. They remind me that even though she is no longer here in the physical sense, her presence remains a guiding force in my life. These experiences have left me with a profound sense of comfort and a belief that our bonds with those we love are unbreakable, enduring beyond the boundaries of time and space. As I close this chapter of memories and reflections, I carry with me the warmth of her spirit, knowing that she continues to watch over me, offering strength and love in ways that words can hardly capture.

Chapter 2
Key Characters

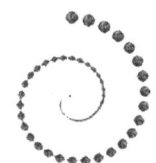

S ome people shape our lives in profound ways, and for me, even though often our relationship was harsh towards one another, no one was more influential than my father. His contrasting world of devotion and complexity laid the foundation for the person I would become. My mother was just 20 when she married my father, who was 10 years her senior. Their relationship was one of contrasts—she was deeply in love and devoted to building a stable family life. He was a charismatic band leader with a reputation as a ladies' man. Despite his charm, my mother remained the steady force in our family, juggling multiple responsibilities with grace. She owned a butcher shop and worked at a textile factory, all while raising children. By the age of 25, she had already given birth to two of my siblings, and the weight of her responsibilities grew heavier. Recognizing the need for support, she made the practical decision to move into a house next to my grandmother's, ensuring she had the help she needed to care for us.

Despite the challenges, she was always a happy, grounded woman who did everything she could to provide for her family.

In the tightly-knit community of our small town, life revolved around the textile factory that had been the heart of the area for generations. Nearly 300 families lived and worked there, forming a large extended family where everyone knew each other intimately. My parents were no exception; their lives intertwined long before they married, as both sets of their parents had also worked at the factory. Growing up in such a close-knit environment, my mother's most significant relationships were undoubtedly with her children. Although she deeply loved my father, their lives took different paths. My father, preferring office work, served as an assistant to a judge, while my mother thrived in the physical work and responsibility of managing our home. Despite their separate worlds, their bond was strong, though it was rarely displayed openly. In our family, love was understood rather than seen, and while I don't recall them showing affection publicly, I do not doubt that my mother loved my father deeply.

My parents shared a deep commitment grounded in their strong religious beliefs and family values. Their bond was undeniable, though their affection was something kept private behind closed doors. In our culture at the time, public displays of affection were seen as disrespectful, and it was customary for couples to express their love only in the privacy of their own space. While this approach was rooted in the values of that era, I believe that things have changed for the better. Today, I think children must witness their parents' love and affection in a healthy, moderate way. It helps them understand the importance of love and connection, and it models positive and healthy relationships for them to carry into their own lives.

According to my elder sister Jeannie, our mother was incredibly lively and affectionate with them whenever she had the time and energy. Despite her busy schedule, she made sure my siblings knew they were loved, always demonstrating her care in both big and small ways. Even while working at the butcher shop, she found opportunities to teach them valuable life lessons. Among many loving days, one that my sister Jeanie recalls and said in her words: "I remember being just four or five years old, sitting outside the shop with our own little table, selling vegetables that she brought from the market. It was her way of instilling independence in us from an early age, teaching us how to stand on our own while still feeling her unwavering support."

As Jeannie continued to share her memories, she painted a picture of our mother as a loving yet firm guide in our lives. While she was incredibly affectionate, she also believed it was her duty to teach us right from wrong, often being strict but always in a gentle and caring manner. We never felt disrespected by her discipline; instead, we understood that it came from a place of love and a desire to help us grow into responsible individuals. My father, on the other hand, was quite different in his approach. He was generally quiet with us, but when he did speak, it was often in moments of anger, asserting his authority in a way that was more intimidating than nurturing. Their contrasting styles left us with two very different models of parenting, each shaping us in unique ways.

My father, despite his emotional reserve, was always there to ensure we had what we needed. Even during the five years we spent in Mexico after my mother passed away, he consistently sent money to support us. He never neglected his responsibilities, even when he was struggling financially. In his own way, he cared deeply for us and tried to show his affection, though he often found it difficult to express. He wasn't always sure how to navigate his role as both mother and father, especially within the expectations of society and his limitations. Still, he did his best to provide and support us.

When my mother died, my father was devastated. He would cry and plead with God, questioning why this tragedy had befallen our family and what he was supposed to do next. The loss left him feeling desperate and overwhelmed. In the months that followed, he grappled with the reality of raising us on his own, even considering allowing others to adopt some of my siblings. But when my grandmother intervened, adamant that we should stay together as a family, he agreed without hesitation. Sending us to live with our grandmother in Mexico was a difficult but wise decision, one rooted in his understanding that it was the best way for us to be surrounded by love and stability while staying with one of the closest family members.

From the moment we arrived at our grandmother's home, she enveloped us in love and provided the security we desperately needed. Though we lived modestly, we never felt deprived because her affection filled our lives with warmth and comfort. Over the next five years, until her passing, she not only nurtured us but also prepared us for the challenges ahead. She taught us essential life skills—how to cook, clean, and manage a household—instilling in us a sense of independence and self-sufficiency. By the time we returned, we were equipped to take care of ourselves, thanks to the foundation she had built.

My sister Jeannie often reminisces about their early childhood prior to my birth. She once told me when they moved to L.A., they didn't have any relatives nearby, but my mom always managed to make friends wherever she went. She continues in her words: "I remember one of her friends would come over, and they would get ready to go out for dinner with my dad. My mom would light up with excitement, like a teenager, as she dressed up for those special occasions. Those were some of the rare moments when I saw her genuinely happy, savoring the joy of a night out. However, there was also a time when things took a darker turn. Once, my mom desperately wanted to get her hair cut because it had grown unruly, but my dad did not have the money for it. Despite her persistent requests, one night, while she was asleep, he took it upon himself to cut her braids off and left her hair short so she would stop asking for money to get it done at the hair salon. She was devastated and cried for weeks afterward; her happiness was overshadowed by that heartbreaking act."

Jeannie took me by my hand and shared some of the happiest memories of their childhood when they first moved to L.A. She said,

"Dad's brother, Uncle Jesse, whenever there were family gatherings or parties, we were always included. Mom, who loved baking, would often bring a birthday cake to these events." Being around my dad's side of the family was a highlight for us, especially since Uncle Jesse had eight children of his own, making for lively and enjoyable times. He was very fond of us and went out of his way to make our visits special, always looking for ways to ensure we had fun. These outings with my mom, dad, and Uncle Jesse's family were some of the most joyful moments we experienced, filled with laughter and the warmth of family connections. Uncle Jesse and his wife, Aunt Terry, went to great lengths to treat us all equally.

Our sister Esperanza, being the oldest, naturally took on a more mature and responsible role. She had a selfless nature, always eager to assist my mom and dad and make life easier for us. Her willingness to help and her dependable presence meant that my parents came to rely heavily on her. While it might have seemed like she was favored, her support was invaluable, and her contributions were a significant source of help and stability for the family.

When I was finally engaged to get married, I felt as if I was jumping into the deep end. Even though I knew my husband as a friend for five years prior to dating, we both attended the same University. Once we began dating, my relationship with him felt like a pair of comfortable slippers—familiar and easy, but still, I was anxious. Our relationship started smoothly because of the friendship we had built, though there were aspects of him that were a bit wild and needed calming down. But as we began our family, any reservations I had were overshadowed by seeing what a wonderful father he was. Despite his own difficult upbringing, with parents who divorced when he was young and a father figure who was absent, he was determined to be a great dad.

He tried to compensate for what he missed in his own childhood by being incredibly attentive to his children. His dedication was evident in the way he showered them with affection and provided for them, sometimes excessively, as we both had good jobs and wanted to make up for our own missed experiences. Watching him embrace and kiss our boys, something that was uncommon in my Mexican culture, and being their unwavering supporter at sports practices and games was truly remarkable. With our daughter, even though he wasn't interested in horses, he supported her passion by ensuring she had a horse and a car when she turned sixteen. His commitment to being an involved and loving father was a sight to behold, and it profoundly impacted on our family life. Our approach to parenting was driven by a desire to provide our children with everything we lacked in our own upbringing. We ensured they had the opportunities and support we did not, which helped them succeed in their careers and education. My daughter, despite the modest financial return from her passion for horses, continues to thrive in what she loves. Overall, we are proud of the upbringing we gave them and seeing them grow into successful, happy individuals.

My sisters and I all followed a similar approach with our own children, striving to give them the opportunities and experiences we missed out on. Each of us wanted to ensure our kids had more than we did. Admittedly, some of us might have spoiled them a bit too much at times, including my brother Tony. But overall, we were united in our goal of providing a better life for the next generation.

Sometimes, I wonder if my mother were still alive, our relationship would have been an ongoing journey of deep connection and shared experiences. I envision us navigating life together, celebrating milestones, and supporting each other through challenges. I would have wanted to involve her in every aspect of my life, from the joys of my successes to the struggles I faced.

I wish I had had her during my formative years and would have grown up having her motherly warmth in my life. As she grew older, our roles would naturally shift. I would take on the responsibility of caring for her, ensuring her comfort and well-being in her later years. I would strive to provide her with the same love, care, and attention she devoted to us. Seeing her as an elderly woman, I would be committed to reciprocating the nurturing and support she gave me, making sure she felt valued and loved every step of the way. It would be my way of honoring all the sacrifices she made for us, ensuring that she could enjoy her later years with the same warmth and security she always provided for her family.

In our culture, the idea of sending a parent to a care facility is rare; instead, we take turns caring for them ourselves. I envision a future where my mom would spend time with each of us in rotation, bringing joy and familial connection into our homes. We would eagerly await our turns to host her, sharing in the responsibility and delight of her presence, making sure she felt cherished and involved in our lives. For instance, during my pregnancies and early motherhood, she would have been a tremendous support, offering her wisdom and love during those demanding times.

Reflecting on other families, like my brother's experience with his mother-in-law, I see a similar pattern of familial care. His mother-in-law, who has lived with them for twelve years, now receives care due to her dementia. This mirrors what I observed growing up in Mexico, where elderly parents were lovingly cared for by their children. It was a cultural norm for parents to be cared for in their later years by the children who had grown up in the same home, ensuring they remained a central, valued part of the family.

This model of care reminds me of one of my elder sister Jeannie's experiences with her mother-in-law. From the time she was 16 while first dating her future first husband-to-be, his mother was a loving presence in her life. Once they were married, her mother-in-law moved in with them during the first four months of giving birth. After both of her pregnancies and even after this first marriage failed, Antonia, her mother-in-law, stayed to help raise her children and provide the maternal care she missed. Her support continued even after she remarried, and she seamlessly integrated into her new family. She became a surrogate mother figure, enriching our lives with her affection and support. The deep bond they shared was a testament to the lasting impact of family love and care, much like what I hope for my relationship with my own mother if she were still with us. My oldest sisters, Espe and Jeannie, took on the responsibility of looking after the younger siblings. As a result, I learned to turn to them for support rather than to my father, with whom I never developed a close bond due to my early separation from dad when we moved to Mexico after mom passed away. I was only six months old, which meant that we missed forming that important bond during the first five years of a child's life. Consequently, I was often afraid of him and avoided interacting with him as much as possible.

Jeannie and her boyfriend, Tavo, filled in for my father in many ways. For example, they attended parent-teacher conferences for me when I was in school, even though Jeannie was only 16 or 17 at the time. My father rarely attended these meetings, so Jeannie and Tavo's involvement was crucial. I remember my teacher recording some of the entire class English assignments for our families to listen to while attending the open house, which Tavo found amusing, much to my embarrassment. Overall, Jeannie and Espe became my mentors and primary sources of support, filling the role my father could not. Espe, the oldest of the siblings, got married at a very young age, much to my father's dismay. For three months leading up to her planned church wedding, my dad tried daily to convince her not to go through with it, unaware that she had already married her husband earlier that summer in Mexico through a civil ceremony. When December came, it was too late—Espe had to go through with the church wedding as planned. Despite my father's initial devastation, the marriage turned out to be a positive development. Her husband, who joined our family after the wedding, ended up being a big help financially and worked well with my dad.

SYLVIA VILLASENOR

Espe's husband always dreamed of returning to Mexico to open a carpenter shop, and after having lived in Los Angeles working very hard and having two children, they eventually moved back when I was 13 in 1972. Espe, a talented cook, also opened a restaurant there. Despite the distance, Espe and I remained very close because she felt a strong sense of duty to care for me, as our mother had asked her to do before she passed away. Espe took this responsibility seriously, looking after me and our younger siblings. Even though she raised nine children of her own in Guadalajara, she continues to visit us twice a year, and our bond remains strong to this day.

Jeannie was always the cheerful and resilient one among us, constantly smiling no matter what challenges she faced. We never saw her cry, even though she might have done so behind closed doors. She was determined to set an example for us, aggressively pursuing her high school education and then quickly moving on to work at White King, a soap factory. Jeannie stepped up to help support us, often buying us clothes and even purchasing tickets for us to spend our summers in Guadalajara—a place we all cherished. Despite her responsibilities, she got married young.

During her dating days with Tavo, they brought a lot of joy and fun into our lives. Tavo had a car and would pack all of us in for trips to Malibu or Griffith Park, followed by a treat at McDonald's, where we enjoyed 25-cent burgers, 10-cent fries, and 5-cent Cokes. Even though I was only six and didn't care much for the music battles between English and Spanish songs in the car, it was clear that Tavo's influence helped us all adapt to life in the U.S. He was smart, spoke perfect English, and had a promising future, eventually going into the military and serving in the Vietnam War. Our time with Tavo, his mom, and his younger brother Bobby—who was hilariously shy and was set up on a date with my sister Ruth. He was so nervous that his hands began to sweat. These memories I have were some of the most fun times of my childhood. Bobby, who later became a priest as his mom had always planned, is still serving the church up to this day. Those were lighthearted and memorable times that we all enjoyed as kids.

Ruth, being the third oldest, had to grow up quickly and take on a lot of responsibilities at an early age. She did not really get to experience much childhood because she was always looking after us—dressing us for school, making our lunches, and more. I vividly remember one time when I was about six years old, waiting for her to help me get dressed for school. She was mad that day and handed me the dress, telling me to do it myself. I did not even know how to get my hands into the sleeves properly, and it hurt my feelings deeply. After that, I knew I needed to keep my distance from her, even though we shared the same bed. She pushed me to become more independent, but it was tough.

One incident that stuck out when I was in the sixth grade. There was an older, scary-looking guy who attended the local Junior High School in our area. He started hanging out outside a small mom-and-pop convenience store located across the street from the grammar school I attended. When school was out, he was there sticking out like a sore thumb and looked very suspicious. I then discovered he was waiting at the corner to spot the first young girl walking home alone. He would proceed to follow them, and I was not sure why, but I ignored it until one day, he started following me. I was scared, but he turned the corner before I got to the top of the hill. I was petrified, so I asked Ruth to please pick me up from school; I told her the reason while I emphasized how frightened I was of this older kid. I asked her, if we saw him, to please stop the car, get out and tell him to stop following me and threaten to report him to our school Principal if he doesn't stop. She reluctantly agreed but emphasized she would do it only for that one time. When we saw the guy, she stopped the car, yelled at him to leave me alone, and then sped off. I was shocked and terrified, thinking that wasn't enough, and sure enough, the older kid followed me again the next day. He grabbed my twelve-year-old behind me and left. After that, he never came back to the school. Ruth was always tough and feisty but also capable of being a lot of fun. She had her own life and got married young, too, so she wasn't always around.

Sheila, the middle child, got married to her first husband when she was twenty-one in August of 1974. This marriage lasted only four years, and she divorced him in 1978. When she moved back home, I was happy to have her back. She succeeded in getting her life back together and obtained a travel agent certificate at our local junior college. Shortly after, on Christmas of 1980, her childhood sweetheart came to the States to visit from Mexico, swapped her off her feet, got married, had a civil court wedding in July of 1981, and moved to Mexico City. They had two children that I did not get to know well during their young years since they lived so far away. She had a good life in Mexico; she was an English school teacher, and her husband worked in his field of civil engineering. He specialized in engineering for building bridges for Mexico City. When her youngest son was eight years old, he was diagnosed with kidney failure. His doctor gave him five years to live with no hope of a transplant. Sheila sold everything they had and moved her family to the States in the hope that her son's life would be saved. I was happy once again to see her move back and find a home to move into with her family near me. My sister, Ruth, helped Sheila obtain medical insurance for her son to get treatment to prepare him for a kidney transplant, and it came through. His older brother was the perfect match and was his donner. Now, both of her children are grown men with successful careers, with families of their own living in the States, and Sheila has four grandchildren. Unfortunately, her husband passed away three years ago. Since I live closest to her, I make sure she knows I'm here for her and my door will always be open. Often, she joins my husband and me out for outings on the weekends, and she is a joy to hang out with.

Tony is my only brother he is about four and a half years older than me. I do not see him much since he lives far from me but close to Jeannie. Tony is very reserved, and I think it is because he had a tough time growing up, Dad was challenging to live with and often bullied him as a child. They struggled to connect when Tony was younger but eventually made amends when Tony finally got married in his early forties. On Tony's wedding day, Dad asked for his forgiveness for trying to mold him into something he wasn't. Tony was always gentle, growing up surrounded by sisters. At one point, I thought he would never marry. When he lived at home, he dated many women, which eventually made him a bit nervous. Despite having girlfriends, he struggled with relationships because they often reminded him of one of us, Jeannie, Ruth, Sheila, Lupe, or me. He finally found the right one that had no personality or physical resemblance to any of his six sisters. His wife Alicia was a girl he met while visiting our town in Mexico during Christmas. She was my cousin Cacho's next-door neighbor. They have been married close to twenty-five years now and have two kids, one still attending Berkeley and the other pursuing pre-med. Both want to become doctors, which makes him proud. Tony is now retired, but he still works remotely as a certified public accountant, a career he has stuck with his entire life. Interestingly, we both graduated from Cal State LA in the same year and month—he went into accounting, and I pursued marketing.

Lupe is the second youngest. I am fourteen months younger than her. Being that we are the closest in age, she and I did everything together and hung out with the same friends from our childhood days in Los Angeles and in Guadalajara up until our teens when she moved away to get married at the age of seventeen. Lupe was your miss popular, many friends, catch you later type of girl. Weekends at home were visited by her friends, who got to know me well, and once I started my first year of High School, I had friends in higher grades on account of her. Lupe's generosity with her friends extended to the extreme of allowing them to wear her clothes to school and mind also. There were a few times that I would bump into her friends at school on my way to one of my classes, and lord and behold, they were wearing my blue jeans. Blue jeans that were not cheap, purchased with my hard-earned money that I worked all summer for. I never confronted her friends at school when I would see them in full bloom wearing my clothes because she had them believe they belonged to her. At home, when I tried to let her have it, all she did was laugh and tell me, "Hush, I'll take you out to eat to make it up to you." "Okay sounds good," would be my answer. Food was the root of all evil; everything was forgiven and forgotten. I cried so much when she left for Guadalajara halfway through her senior year of High School to get married. Her future husband was a young well, known professional soccer player who played for one of the two professional soccer teams of Guadalajara, "Atlas." he was recruited by a coach who was also from our hometown. His name is Bernardino Garcia and he is five years her senior. Financially, Lupe would be well, so Dad did not object at all when she left to get married at a young age. Lupe had a good life with Berna. They had two children that were born and raised in Guadalajara. Unfortunately, professional athletic careers are often short-lived, and if the money earned is invested in the wrong investments, you can lose it all. This happened to Lupe and her husband, and they had to move to the States to start over from ground zero. Lupe is a sharp person and quickly regained her aggressiveness in job searching, and was also able to get permanent residence for her husband and two children. It was hard for the family to move here due to the culture shock along with having to leave friends and family behind, but the need to survive was a priority, and the States is where to begin if that is the case. They both were placed in jobs with the help of friends, and her children eventually got used to life here, blessed with great careers. Lupe and her husband, Berna, retired and moved back to Guadalajara. Berna coached a youth team of boys from twelve and up who have the potential to turn professional. Berna is now fully retired, and Lupe works remotely from home part-time to supplement their retirement income.

As for the rest of us, I think we were all raised with a strong sense of independence. Each of us tried to forge our own path, and now, as adults, we've all had good careers and are able to support ourselves without relying on anyone else. Despite our independence, we've always tried to stay close as siblings. When we were younger and married, raising our kids, we used to get together once a month to celebrate everyone's birthdays. Those gatherings kept us connected and strengthened our bond.

But as time went on and our families grew, it became harder to find a place big enough for all of us to meet. Now, we still come together for special occasions—weddings, funerals, or just the occasional visit with one or two siblings.

Esperanza, our oldest sister, naturally took on the role of the mother figure in our family. Even though we all knew she was our sister, she was the one we turned to when we needed support. No matter where she was, even if she was in Mexico, she would fly back to be with us during both the good and bad times. Her own children sometimes resented the attention she gave us, but they've come to understand that she loved us all equally.

MAMA'S PEARLS

Esperanza was determined to be independent from a young age. She got a job while still in high school and was always competitive with Jeannie, which she encouraged because it made her stronger. Esperanza married before finishing high school and started her family early. Despite the challenges, we've remained close, calling each other often. Ruth is battling Parkinson's but is doing well under the circumstances. She knows that we are there for her for support and take her out whenever we can. Next is Sheila. From the moment she was born, she had this fiery personality—she would get angry over the smallest things and was the type of child who, if she got mad, would do something drastic like putting her face in puddles after it rained in Mexico. On the other hand, Sheila was and still is very creative, she loved putting on shows for the kids that lived on Nina Jose's block and would charge a small admission fee. Nina Jose's patio would fill up and her shows were always a success.

Tony, our brother, was quite the opposite. He never liked playing soccer or joining in the outdoor games with the other kids. After our mother passed away, Tony went through a period of depression. He spent most of his time sitting at grandmother's feet as she sat in her special chair because she couldn't walk. She tried her best to lift his spirits, encouraging him to go out and play, but he struggled more than the rest of us for admission. We learned to work with her quirks and love her creative spirit.

While we found friends quickly and moved on with our lives, based on Jeannie's observation, Tony remained reserved, preferring solitude over socializing. Eventually, he did start making friends, but he never had as many as we did. Our father, seeing Tony as the only boy, believed that being tough on him would help him grow into a proper man. This approach caused Tony a lot of pain, but he used it as motivation to better himself. He went to college, landed a great job, and built a successful life.

In the end, Tony's determination paid off. He eventually got married and now has a wonderful family. His wife has never had to work, and he continues to support them, wanting to keep working until their kids become doctors. I'm very proud of him for everything he's achieved. Lupe was the one my mom put Jeannie in charge of, so she always tried her best to be there for her.

As for Jeannie and me, we have a great relationship. We call each other whenever something's going on with us or our families, and we often go on vacations together. I love her kids and her husband, and we've always gotten along well. I don't think we've ever had a fight.

Jeannie says my brother Tony always tried to keep his distance from our dad because Dad was constantly criticizing him. No matter what my brother accomplished, Dad never acknowledged the good, only the bad. From a young age, my brother's manhood was questioned. Dad thought he was too wimpy and skinny and would even tell him that he was going to get a couple of guys to fight him to see how much of a man he was. My brother was just 10 or 11 at the time, and he couldn't understand why Dad treated him that way.

As a result, my brother would sometimes take out his frustrations on Lupe and me because we were younger and had nothing to do with the situation. It wasn't fair, but it was his way of coping. After Dad's second wife left him, they had to share a bedroom. Tony lasted about a week before he moved back to the couch, saying that Dad snored too much and yelled in his sleep. Over time, as they both got older, they began to understand each other a little better. They developed a sort of man-to-man relationship, and eventually, they were on better terms. Unfortunately, I never had that kind of conversation with Dad. It wasn't until after I got married and spent more time around him that he finally started being nice to me, but even then, we never got close since he retired and moved to Mexico.

My sister Ruth once confronted Dad after he had a child with a girlfriend in Mexico when he was in his late 60s. He married her, and he was so loving and attentive to their daughter, always hugging and kissing her, taking her everywhere. Ruth couldn't understand why he was so affectionate with this child when he had never shown us that kind of love. She asked him why he kept his distance from us when we wanted to be close to him. That's when Dad explained why he felt he needed to keep his distance, and that was how we finally understood his behavior.

Jeannie shared something with me that happened the day before Mom went to the hospital. The doctor thought she had a fallen uterus from having so many kids so close together, but it turned out to be her appendix. Mom had a premonition that she was going to die. We tried to reassure her, saying it was just a fallen uterus, no big deal, but she felt it was more serious. That's when she talked to my sister Esperanza and me together. She told Esperanza that if anything happened to her, she needed to be responsible for the younger siblings, especially Sylvia, who was just a baby at the time. Mom said Sylvia would require a lot of attention and made Esperanza promise to make sure everyone treated her right and that she would make it through. Then she turned to me and said that I would be in charge of Lupe, who was only a year and a half old. Mom wanted to ensure that Lupe would always be okay and that no one would mistreat her.

We have held on to that responsibility closely ever since. Even today, we still take Mom's words to heart, making sure that we take care of each other as she asks.

Sometimes, Jeannie and I mentally revisit the Sunday mornings after Mass. They were special. If we could not make it to the park because my dad didn't have a car, we would just gather in the front yard. She would sit with us, and we would talk about all sorts of things, like what we wanted to be when we grew up. Those moments were so meaningful because she would encourage us to think about our futures and dream big. This was when we were already here, living on Irola Street. She says she remembered me being in a stroller, and so did another one of us. We would all sit there together, having these deep conversations with her.

My mother always emphasized the importance of independence. She would tell us, "I don't want you to ever rely on anybody for your well-being. Even if you marry a rich person, I want you to work." She wanted each of us to be self-sufficient, to buy our own cars, and to have good jobs. It was something she and her mother talked to us about often, instilling those values in us from an early age. And she never failed to remind us that no matter what, she would always love us. She reassured us that wherever she was, she would be with us, watching over us. Those words have stayed with me all my life.

Chapter 3
Setting the Stage

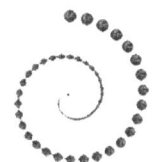

As said by one of the famous German American Physiologist, Martin H. Fischer, *"All the world is a laboratory to the inquiring mind."* For me, this sentiment rang true from an early age. My childhood was a tapestry of curiosity, woven with endless questions and discoveries. I sought to understand the complexities of my father and the intricate dance of life's difficulties in Mexico and the United States. Every experience was a piece of a larger puzzle, urging me to explore, learn, and uncover the secrets of the world around me. My childhood was spent in Guadalajara. It was where my story began, in a town where the streets were narrow but full of life, and the church wasn't just a place we visited—it was a constant presence woven into the rhythm of our days. Every morning, the bells would ring, their sound echoing through the cobblestone streets, calling us to prayer, to community, to the familiar faces that greeted us with smiles and nods as we walked by. This small town, nestled in the heart of Mexico, was more than just a place to live; it was a sanctuary, a place where everyone knew each other, where faith wasn't just practiced on Sundays but lived every day.

Life in Guadalajara was simple, but it was rich in ways that words often fail to capture. There was a sense of belonging, a deep connection to not only the people but to the land, to the traditions, and especially to the church. The church wasn't just where we went to mass; it was the center of our lives. Everything revolved around it—the baptisms, the weddings, the funerals, even the fiestas. Faith wasn't something we questioned; it was something we breathed in and out every day.

My paternal grandmother would take me to mass almost daily, and I remember how the light filtered through the stained glass, casting colorful patterns on the church walls. The air was always heavy with incense, and the sound of whispered prayers filled the space. I felt safe there, as if nothing in the outside world could touch us as long as we were within those sacred walls. The priest's voice, deep and calm, was a constant in my life, a reminder that no matter what happened, we had the church, and we had each other.

We really, really enjoyed life there. There was something magical about the simplicity of it all—how everyone knew everyone, how we were all bound together by the same beliefs, the same rituals. The food we ate, the way we celebrated, the way we mourned—it was all the same. There was comfort in that sameness, a kind of warmth that I would come to miss more than I realized.

Then came the day when everything changed. We moved back to

the States, and suddenly, the world was five times bigger. It was overwhelming in a way that I can't fully describe. I remember arriving at our new home in Los Angeles and feeling as if I had been dropped into a completely different universe. The buildings were taller, the streets wider, and the people—there were so many people, and they all looked different. It was like nothing I had ever seen before.

I was just a child then, too young to fully understand what was happening but old enough to feel the weight of it. The world that had once been so small, so familiar, was now vast and unknown. Everything felt bigger—too big, too fast, too much. I had no choice but to adapt. Little by little, I began to dissect this new world, trying to make sense of it, trying to find my place in it.

The church was still there, but it wasn't the same. In Guadalajara, faith was woven into every part of our lives, but here, it seemed to be something people did on Sundays and then forgot about for the rest of the week. We still went to church, but it didn't feel as deep and all-encompassing as it was in Guadalajara. It was just another building, another place to go, rather than the center of our world. But even so, my family made sure that faith remained a part of our daily lives. Every night before bed, we prayed together, my older sisters leading the way. And every morning before we left for school, we prayed again, asking for protection, guidance, and strength.

But the world outside our home was different. It wasn't just Mexicans anymore: people who looked like us, who believed like us, who lived like us. There were so many different kinds of people—different faces, different languages, different foods, different everything. I had never imagined that so many different kinds of people could exist in one place. At school, I found myself surrounded by kids who didn't speak Spanish and who didn't know the first thing about the life I had left behind. It was like being dropped into a foreign land without a map, and I was left to figure it out on my own.

At first, it was hard. I missed the comfort of Guadalajara, the way everything felt familiar and safe. I missed the church, the way it had been the center of everything. I missed the way life made sense. But as time went on, I started to adapt. I began to see that this new world, as strange and overwhelming as it was, had its own kind of beauty. There were things here that I had never experienced before, things that challenged me and that made me grow.

I started to dissect every part of our new environment, trying to make sense of it all. I began to see that this new place, with all its differences, wasn't something to be feared but something to be explored. I learned that people could be different in a million ways but still be kind, still be good, and still be worth knowing. I learned that there was more than one way to live, more than one way to believe, more than one way to be.

And through it all, my family remained my anchor. My sisters, especially, were a constant source of strength for me. They guided me through prayers, through school, and through the challenges of adapting to a new life. They helped me hold on to the values we had brought with us from Guadalajara, even as we learned to navigate this new world. And in the end, it was that balance—between holding on to our roots and embracing the new—that helped me find my way.

Looking back now, I can see that both worlds—the one I left behind in Guadalajara and the one I came to know in the States—shaped who I am today. They taught me that faith, family, and community are what matter most, no matter where you are. They taught me that life is full of changes, but it's the values you carry with you that keep you grounded. And they taught me that, even when the world feels too big, too fast, too much, there is always a way to find your place in it.

Adjusting to life in the States was a culture shock at first. Everything seemed so different—the language, the people, the way things worked. I remember feeling out of place like I was on the outside looking in. But as time went on and I began to understand the language, I started to realize that maybe things weren't so different after all. Once I got to know the people around me, I found that, in many ways, they were a lot like me. Sure, they might have looked different or eaten different foods at home—some came from parts of the world I had only heard about—but deep down, we were all just kids trying to make sense of the world.

I remember making friends and discovering that we shared the same fears and the same joys. We were afraid of not fitting in, of failing our tests, of disappointing our families. We laughed at the same jokes, played the same games, and looked forward to recess with the same excitement. It didn't matter where we came from or what language we spoke at home; we were all in the same boat, navigating the ups and downs of growing up.

Many of my classmates had been born and raised in the States, so they were ahead of me in their studies. They didn't have the language barrier to overcome, and they seemed so confident, so sure of themselves. For me, it was a struggle just to keep up, to understand what the teacher was saying, to follow along in class. But instead of feeling defeated, I saw them as role models. They were who I wanted to be—fluent in the language, knowledgeable in the subjects, and comfortable in this new world. So, I worked hard to catch up, determined to be like them and to belong in the same way they did.

Another part of adjusting to this new life was the food. In Mexico, we have always eaten traditional Mexican meals—tortillas, beans, rice and salsas in assorted colors and textures that give our dishes a unique flavor. But here, I was introduced to foods I had never even heard of before. Chinese food, Italian food, pizza—these were things that were completely foreign to me at first but quickly became part of our fun. I remember how excited we would get when my older sisters, who had started working and making their own money, would take us out to eat. It was a treat, not just because of the food but because it was time spent together, exploring this new world of flavors without the presence of our father. We would walk to nearby restaurants, laughing and talking, savoring the freedom that came with those moments.

SYLVIA VILLASENOR

One of the biggest differences between life in Mexico and life in the States was the sense of independence we were pushed to develop. In Mexico, especially as girls, we were sheltered. There was always someone watching over us, making sure we didn't stray too far and that we stayed within the boundaries that were considered safe. We weren't encouraged to explore the world on our own; in fact, it was often discouraged. We were taught that the world could be a dangerous place, especially for girls, and that it was better to stay close to home, where we would be protected.

But in the States, things were different. From an early age, we were encouraged to be independent and to find our own way. Opportunities to work to make money came early, and with that came a sense of responsibility that we had not experienced before. My sisters started working as soon as they were old enough, earning their own money and learning to navigate the world on their own. It was not always easy, but it was empowering. It was a chance to step out of the sheltered life we had known in Mexico and start building our own paths.

That push towards independence changed me. It forced me to grow up faster, to learn how to take care of myself, and to find my own way in a world that was still so new and unfamiliar. But it also gave me confidence, a sense of strength that I hadn't known I had. It showed me that I could handle more than I had ever imagined and that I was capable of more than I had ever been given credit for. And it taught me that, even in a world that seemed so different, there was always a way to find common ground, connect with others, and create a home outside your homeland.

The memories of walking to school at the age of ten overwhelm me when I look back. I was scared to go out and face the world all by myself. As Ralph Waldo Emerson said, *"The only person you are destined to become is the person you decide to be."* I overcame my fears and threw myself out. That decision made me stronger than I have ever thought I could be. I wonder if I hadn't done it that time, I wouldn't be the person I am today.

I remember the summer when I was just 14, two years before I was even legally old enough to work. By then, I had seen my older sisters go off to their jobs, earning their own money and gaining a sense of independence that fascinated me. I watched closely, paying attention to how they approached work and how they managed their time. It was not about making money; it was about stepping into the world on their own terms, and I was eager to do the same. I had seen the confidence it gave them, the way it changed their lives, and I wanted that, too.

So, even though I was still a couple of years away from being 16—the age when most kids could start working legally—I decided to find a job for myself. I knew the drill by then. I had observed how my sisters handled themselves, how they approached people for work, how they made their own way. I knew it would not be easy, especially since I didn't have the advantage of being brought into a job by a sibling. It only happened once or twice when one of my sisters would take me along and help me get hired at a place where they already worked. But for the most part, I was on my own. And that was a challenge.

But it was also exciting. I remember the thrill of getting that first job and the pride I felt when I was able to work during the summer and earn my own money. It was a small step, but it meant everything to me. When school started back up, I kept working part-time, balancing my schoolwork with my new responsibilities. It wasn't always easy, but I was determined to make it work. I liked the feeling of independence and the sense of control over my own life. It was something new, something I hadn't experienced in the same way before.

Looking back, I realize that those early jobs, those first steps into the working world, played a significant role in shaping who I became. They pushed me to be independent and to embrace the changes and challenges that came with life in a new country. Up until the age of five, my life had been in Mexico, surrounded by family, tradition, and a world that felt familiar. But when we moved back to the States, I was thrown into a completely different reality— one that was bigger, more complex, and full of new possibilities.

Even though I was born in the USA, I had only spent the first five months of my life there before moving to Guadalajara, Mexico. It wasn't until I was five years old that we returned, and it felt like I was starting over in a place that was supposed to be home but still felt foreign. But as I grew older, I began to understand that maybe this was where I was meant to be all along. The struggles, the challenges, the new experiences—they were all part of what was molding me into the person I was becoming.

MAMA'S PEARLS

That sense of independence and learning to navigate the world on my own was something that stuck with me. It was different from the life I had known in Mexico, where everything was more sheltered and more controlled. Here, I was being pushed to grow up faster, take on responsibilities, and figure things out for myself. And as difficult as that was at times, it also gave me a sense of strength and purpose. It taught me that I could handle whatever came my way, that I could adapt to new circumstances, and that I had a place in this world, even if it didn't always feel that way at first.

So, while my early years in Mexico had been full of love and tradition, my life in the States was teaching me a different set of lessons—lessons about independence, patience, and finding my way in a world that was constantly changing. And as much as I missed the simplicity of life in Guadalajara, I began to embrace the differences, realizing that they were shaping me into someone who could thrive in this new environment.

Reflecting on my journey so far, I feel a sense of gratefulness that I got the opportunity to live my life here in the States. A profound nostalgia washes over me whenever I step foot in Mexico, a tangible echo of the life I once knew, the life that I left behind. People, places, and cultures bring back all the happy and sad memories, and I cherish the vibe of just being there. However, if I look back at my childhood when I spent my summers in Mexico, I love that feeling. I used to think that it was home. I would always look to come back to where my people were. There was a comforting embrace of home that enveloped me. Two of my sisters were married and lived there.

SYLVIA VILLASENOR

Once, it was believed that one cannot leave their homeland, and Mexico was it for us but time has changed that.

The neighborhood in Guadalajara where we lived was small but lively. Imagine a block with maybe 22-24 houses—10-12 on each side of the street and two more up at the top. The blocks were short, so in about 15 minutes, you could easily walk around one part of town. Every corner of that town seemed familiar, but nothing was as deeply embedded in my memory as my paternal grandmother's house.

Her home stood on one of those blocks, and even now, the details of it are etched in my mind as vividly as if I were walking through it today. You'd enter through a metal door, which led into a small patio. In that patio stood a tree that bore sweet limes. I remember that tree, the way its branches would sway gently in the breeze, and the way its fruit smelled in the sun. Underneath that tree was a stone sink—though calling it just a sink doesn't do it justice. It was made of rock, with one deep basin to hold water and a sloped side where clothes were scrubbed. It wasn't uncommon for people in the neighborhood to wash their clothes this way since many didn't have washing machines back then. My grandmother didn't, either.

I can still see her standing there, scrubbing clothes on that rough stone, her hands moving with the familiarity of a routine that she had done countless times. She never let me help, though. I was too young, and she always had my older cousins or other family members to lend a hand. After the clothes were washed, we would hang them upstairs to dry. In homes like my grandmother's, unless you had a second story with rooms, the rooftop was the drying space, where clotheslines stretched from one end to the other, catching the sun.

The layout of her house was simple but practical, built for the flow of family life. To the left of the patio was the bathroom—still technically outside but within the confines of the house. Next was the kitchen, where my grandmother always seemed to be preparing something. It had everything you needed, even though it was modest. Past the kitchen was the dining room and then a set of stairs leading up to the rooftop, where we hung the laundry.

Downstairs, to the right, was the living room—a fairly large space, though much of it was taken up by twin beds. Those beds were always ready for family members who came to stay, and one of them became mine whenever we visited. Another bedroom branched off from the living room, where two of my cousins stayed with my grandmother. The house was always full of women; this included my grandmother's daughters, who came to visit on a daily basis—strong, determined women who took care of their homes and their young ones and, in addition, made sure that their mother's household ran smoothly.

These women—my grandmother, my aunts, and my cousins—were the heart of that house. They filled it with warmth and laughter, and they taught us the values that shaped us. They were caretakers, not just of the home, but of our hearts and minds, instilling in us the strength and resilience we would carry into the world.

SYLVIA VILLASENOR

Even now, that house holds a special place in my memory. It still exists, though it's no longer my rest haven when I visit. After my grandmother passed, they divided it in half—one part for the cousin who had stayed with her all those years and the other half for me. But at 22, I was too young and didn't have the means to take care of it. I didn't need the house, and I didn't have the resources to maintain it, so I passed it on to another cousin who was about to get married. It felt right at the time, but that house, with its stone sink and sweet lime tree, will always be a part of me.

The house in Guadalajara, the one my grandmother left behind, is now occupied by one of her great-grandsons, who is raising his family there. It's comforting to know that life continues within those walls and that the warmth of family remains even after all these years. Many of the homes in that neighborhood were similar— modest yet filled with character and life. Over time, people have added second stories, making their homes larger and, in some cases, nicer. But not all of them have held up. Some are falling apart, and neglected as time moves on. Often, the parents have passed away, and without solid documents to pass the house on, they've been left empty and abandoned.

Despite that, the streets outside those homes were always full of life when I was growing up. We would play outside with the neighborhood kids, running up and down the block until 10 o'clock at night, and we were safe. Even at that hour, you could still hear laughter echoing through the streets as children played under the dim streetlights. At 10, though, everyone knew it was time to go inside. It was a small town where you could walk to the store or a relative's house, even at nine at night, without fear. It felt like home—warm, safe, familiar.

Coming to the big city of Los Angeles was a shock. As soon as the sun set, fear crept in. You could not be outside after dark, not alone, at least. The streets were different here—quieter, but in a way that felt dangerous. There were times when we had come home from downtown, and as a kid, I'd step off the bus and run down the street if it were dark, heart pounding because you never knew what could happen. There was always a sense of someone lurking, ready to steal your purse or worse. It wasn't like Guadalajara, where the streets were alive and you felt secure.

The houses were different, too. The homes we grew up in, along with the three rental homes we lived in before my dad finally bought a house, were all small wood cottage homes built in the 1900s. The home Dad finally was able to purchase in the summer of 1968 was a three-bedroom house with a spacious living room when you walked in a dining table for six behind it; two of the three bedrooms were located on the right side of the living room and dining area, the kitchen was next through a door right behind the dining room, a door that always remained open. To the right of the kitchen was the bathroom. Behind the kitchen was another door that led to a hallway; the back door was to the left, and the laundry room was on the right side. Passing the hallway was the final third bedroom where Dad and my brother Tony slept. Tony hated that room so much that he ended up sleeping on the couch in the living room instead.

SYLVIA VILLASENOR

The backyard was small; the two-car garage was next to it. My dad had a green thumb and loved to plant things. He created a beautiful garden in the back and front yard of the house. People in the neighborhood would often stop to admire the front garden. That house, in its own way, was home too. But it wasn't the same kind of home as the ones in Mexico. There was something missing, a certain warmth. Maybe it was the people who made the difference. In Guadalajara, it was my paternal grandmother, aunts, and cousins— strong women who filled the house with love and life. In L.A., it was just us, and while it was home, it felt colder, more distant. My dad tried, but he had it hard, and it reflected in how we all lived. Still, we always had that home, even if it didn't carry the same feeling of comfort that we had known in Mexico. It was warm, homely, something that stays with you like the tangible feeling of holding it in your hands. Growing up, life in Mexico revolved around family, the church, and the rhythms of work. The fathers were usually the breadwinners, though some mothers worked too. What made life in Mexico unique were the frequent holidays that allowed families to truly spend time together. I don't know if they still have it, but back then, many factories will close for two weeks around Christmas. This break gave families the chance to be together, enjoying the holiday season. After Christmas, many families would head to the beach, whether by car or bus, staying in modest hotels depending on what they could afford. But as a child, none of that mattered—being with family, eating out, exploring new places, and swimming in the warm water was what made those trips special. The weather between October and February was ideal for beach outings before the heat became unbearable.

Easter was another major holiday when people took time off. It was two weeks of vacation, the first of which was dedicated to observing Holy Week, remembering the events leading up to Christ's death. This was a deeply religious time, marked by rituals and closeness to the church. After the solemnity of Holy Week, the second week was a time for relaxation and celebration, often spent back at the beach or visiting family. Some people even traveled to the United States or Mexico City if they had family there.

Independence Day, on the 15th of September, was another big occasion. Many people confuse it with Cinco de Mayo, but that's just a minor celebration of a single battle against the French. Independence Day is when Mexico celebrates its freedom from Spanish colonization with pride and patriotism. These holidays and traditions were woven into the fabric of our lives, bringing families together and reinforcing our connection to our heritage.

In Mexico, family time and traditions were deeply cherished. Independence Day, celebrating liberation from the Spaniards, was a major event. We had an entire week off, and it was a time for family gatherings, laughter, and plenty of food. In Guadalajara, and in many parts of Mexico, the main meal of the day was between 1 to 3 p.m. Our family always sat down together at 2 p.m., sharing stories, laughing, and enjoying each other's company. Those meals were the heart of our connection.

I remember fondly the time spent with my mom's side of the family. Her brother, his wife, and the one cousin I have on mom's side always included Sheila, Tony, Lupe, and me in their family Holiday festivities and outings when we spent our summer vacation in Guadalajara. My mom's sister, Nina Jose, would take us downtown Guadalajara to buy us shoes and clothes and then treat us to eat at a restaurant before heading back home. By 7 p.m., the streets would come alive, and everyone would be out enjoying snacks from vendors. Food was a central part of life there, and it made those moments feel even richer.

Coming to the U.S., though, was different. Here, life is more fast-paced, and there isn't as much time to spend with family. If you're working, you're lucky if you get the 24th off for Christmas, the 25th for Christmas Day, and then you're back to work on the 26th. New Year's and Easter are the same. The demands of work in the U.S. make it hard to find quality time with family. Even though you might be better off financially, the time you spend with your kids here doesn't compare to what we had in Mexico.

Here, families often grow up with older siblings looking after the younger ones because the parents are busy working to make ends meet. On weekends, you might get a day to go to church, a park, or the beach if you are lucky. But it's a rat race—groceries to get, kids to prepare, and never enough time. The trade-off is that vacations here can be incredible. You can take nice trips, visit family in Mexico, or go on cruises that were out of reach when we were kids. The dollar goes further when you visit, and you can do things that are now more affordable.

But the difference in lifestyle is stark. In Mexico, everything revolves around family and community. Here, as you get older, you spend more time with friends from work or school because you see them more often than your own family. Weekends become time spent with friends instead of family. The distance between homes can be 25, 30, or even 40 minutes, so it's not like Mexico, where everyone lives close by and you could easily visit.

Yet, there's something to be said about balancing the best of both worlds. You take what you can from each experience and make the most of it, adapting to the life and opportunities that each place offers. But even with that balance, there are moments when you can't help but feel the weight of what's been lost—those fleeting moments of warmth, of togetherness, that no amount of success or distance can ever bring back. You move forward, carrying the echoes of that laughter, those meals shared, and the sense of home that lingers long after the doors have closed.

I think that when you grow up with a family that carries values from their ancestry, and they hold onto them and pass them on, it becomes something truly special. It's like having a roadmap guiding you to where you want to be and the values you want to pass on to your children. For us, that foundation came from our grandmothers, who were such a big part of our lives when we lived in Mexico. They instilled in us a deep sense of family, faith, and tradition—values that shaped us, just as they shaped our cousins on my dad's side, who were raised in the same town. These beliefs, especially the importance of God and prayer, became the cornerstone of our lives.

SYLVIA VILLASENOR

Even during the rebellious teenage years or those confusing times in our twenties, those values stayed with us, silently guiding our decisions. You see others living with what seems like boundless freedom, doing things without a second thought, and you wonder why you're not like them. You try to fit in, to explore that kind of freedom, but something always pulls you back. You realize that you were raised differently, with a different moral compass, and that compass doesn't let you stray too far.

I tried to pass those values on to my children. At times, it seemed like they weren't listening, but as they grew older, I saw how much they absorbed. That strong influence from family, constantly reminding us to stay on the right path, left an impact on them, too.

But there was another side to my upbringing. Growing up in the States, I became more independent than I ever would have been if I had stayed in Mexico. Living here opened up new avenues for me, showing me that women could make it too—that it wasn't just men who had to be the breadwinners. Being here changed my perspective. It gave me the confidence to believe that I could stand on my own two feet and that I didn't have to depend on a man for security. Family values remained at the core of who I was, but the independence I gained here gave me the strength to know that if life ever took an unexpected turn, I would be okay on my own.

Getting my career, earning my own income, and knowing that if my marriage didn't work out, I would be okay—and so would my children—was important to me. But I also realized that no one was going to hand me that security on a silver platter. I had to build it myself. My family was always there, but not in a way that was overly supportive emotionally or financially. It was more like silent encouragement, watching how my sisters navigated their lives, especially after their own marriages ended.

Two of my older sisters got married young, long before they were truly ready. They went through painful divorces and had to become independent, figuring out how to be the sole providers for their children. Watching them made me determined not to follow the same path too quickly. It wasn't jealousy I felt—on the contrary, I had a deep empathy for them. They had to struggle, rebuild, and become stronger in the face of hardship. Ruth, another sister, had a husband who became severely depressed after losing his job. She took charge, working full-time to support their family until he could get back on his feet.

Seeing all of this, I knew I didn't want to rush into marriage. I wanted to be prepared, financially and emotionally, to face whatever life threw at me. My father's push for me to get married young, to be the last one settled so he could feel that his work was done, weighed on me. But I resisted, with the support of my grandmother, who helped him see that I needed time. That was a relief, and while I saw my sisters doing okay in the end, I still wanted to make sure that my story would be different.

Watching my older sisters navigate their lives taught me so much. It was not about following their footsteps—it was about learning from their choices, both the good and the difficult ones. I saw their strength and resilience, but I also saw the struggles that came with getting married young and unprepared. I admired their morals and how they carried themselves before marriage, and I wanted to emulate that. I wanted to avoid getting into trouble at a young age, like some of the girls I saw around me.

One lesson that stayed with me happened when I was 14. I took a summer job through our local High School program, where I lied about my age to get a work permit. My sister helped me with that, and I ended up working at a nonprofit organization, stuffing envelopes. It seemed like a simple, straightforward job, but the experience left a lasting impact on me. There were other students there, but three of the girls were from a home for pregnant teenagers. They were just a few years older than me, maybe 15, 16, and 17. One had already given up her baby for adoption, another was about to give birth, but the third girl... her story shook me to my core.

She was seven months pregnant, angry, and heartbroken because her boyfriend hadn't come to see her for a few weeks. She then found out he had been dating someone else for a much longer time than her. She was devastated. So, she stopped showing up to work and never returned. When I asked the other girls what had happened, they told me she had tried to abort her baby with a wire hanger in the bathtub and lost the baby. This was done out of spite and anger.

Hearing that sent chills down my spine. I had already visited their home and seen how they lived—a big house with six rooms, two girls per room. But learning what she had done made me realize how fragile life can be, especially at that age. I couldn't imagine going through something like that, and it became a turning point for me. I vowed never to let that happen to me. I didn't have my mom or dad close by to guide me, and the thought of mindlessly ending up in a similar situation terrified me.

Seeing what that girl went through made me stronger. It was a lesson I took to heart: to be careful with my choices, to value myself, and never to let anger or hurt push me into a decision I couldn't take back. That moment sealed my resolve to chart a different path for myself.

When we first moved here, it wasn't long before we found ourselves in the middle of significant historical events. In 1968, shortly after we had settled in, riots erupted because of the civil rights movement, which was gaining momentum. The assassination of Martin Luther King Jr. in April that year sent shockwaves through the Black community and the entire nation. Even though many likely anticipated that something like this could happen, it was still a devastating moment. It deeply affected our school and the Black teachers there, leaving everyone shaken.

Just two months later, in June of that same year, right before our school closed for the summer, Robert Kennedy was assassinated at the Ambassador Hotel, only a few miles from my school. That hotel has since been torn down and replaced by a high school. My father, a staunch Democrat who admired the Kennedy family, was deeply affected by this tragedy. The political climate was tense and chaotic, and I was just nine years old, trying to make sense of it all.

We were scared. We didn't fully understand what was happening, but we felt fear in the air. My dad was anxious, too, and that made things even more unsettling. We were living through history, but at the time, it just felt like uncertainty and fear. I remember hearing on the news that we should sleep with our shoes on, ready to run if our house was set on fire during the riots. The riots weren't that close to us, but as a kid, the thought of something like that happening was terrifying.

That year, 1968, was one of the hardest. We had just moved here, and suddenly, we were living through major events that would go down in history. Looking back, I realize that we were part of that history, even if we were just bystanders. The lesson I learned from that time is that people will fight for their rights, even if it means risking their lives. That was the reality of the world we were in, and it left a lasting impression on me.

My dad was a Democrat, deeply committed to the Democratic Party, largely because of his financial status. He believed that Democrats offered more support to the families that financially struggled, like us—compared to Republicans, who, in his view, often took a "find your own way" approach. During Republican administrations, he noticed that resources for people with less were often cut, making life even more difficult for those already struggling. Labor work paid enough to pay the bills and bring food to the table.

He was a huge fan of Robert Kennedy because he saw in him a continuation of what his brother, John F. Kennedy, had tried to do during his presidency. My dad probably benefited from those policies, and he appreciated leaders who advocated for people in need. He also admired Martin Luther King Jr., who had the courage to lead his people through such a tumultuous time, fighting against years of oppression.

This admiration for leaders who stood up for the marginalized influenced all of us. We saw the world through his eyes, and we grew up valuing those who extended a helping hand to those who needed it most. My dad's beliefs made a lasting impact on our family, shaping our values and our outlook on life.

In the summer of 1976, I was 17 and desperately seeking a summer job to buy clothes because, come September, when school started, I would be in my senior year of high school. I was fortunate to find a job right away at a department store not too far from home. It was an exclusive specialty store named Bullock's Wilshire. The store sold soft goods only, such as clothing, perfumes, stationery, and silverware, excluding hard goods such as appliances or furniture. I got hired immediately as a part-time "floater," meaning I would move from department to department based on their needs.

The first department I was assigned to was the Playdeck, located on the mezzanine level. The stock person had gone on vacation for two weeks and the department manager was desperate for a temporary stock girl. The buyer of that department was a woman who traveled the world searching for exclusive merchandise and was known for being extremely demanding. She was away the first week I worked there but was due to return the second week when I would be assigned to work on the Playdeck. The salespeople and assistant buyers taught me how to manage the various clothing brands they carried—luxury items that catered to elderly travelers, with pants priced at $92 and jackets at $300. My job was to keep the dressing rooms clean and get the clothes back out on the floor quickly.

When the buyer returned the second week and stepped out of her office to meet her temporary stock girl, just to make sure I was doing my job right. Lord, have mercy on me. She caught me sitting in the middle of the stockroom a few minutes after I had just gotten back from my lunch break. In my defense, the stock room was a mess, and I was overwhelmed, trying to figure out how to organize the 70 pieces of merchandise to make it easier to get it out the fastest. The buyer was a short Cuban lady with a loud voice and a thick accent. She absolutely let me have it, telling me that if I didn't have the stockroom cleaned in half an hour, she would send me down to HR, and she would make sure that I would never work there again. She scared me so much, that after she left stomping her Italian boots on the floor. I quickly got to work, zipping and buttoning every piece of merchandise up, and with the help of the sales ladies, we were done in 20 minutes. Once she came back within 25 minutes and checked the condition of the stock room, her jaw drooped. She looked at me with awe and I apologized; something changed after that. She looked at me and apologized to me too. After, she asked me to follow her to the floor to help her with the displays. She began to talk to me in Spanish and took me under her wing after that. She was married with no children in her early forties and told me that she was my Tia Magda; Tia means auntie in Spanish.

MAMA'S PEARLS

This woman became my mentor. She taught me everything I needed to know about the business and encouraged me to continue my education. I ended up attending the Fashion Institute to study Merchandising, which later encouraged me to transfer to Cal State LA to get my bachelor's degree in marketing. Once I transferred to the University, I got promoted to sales, where I could also earn a commission to help cover my tuition and books. Shortly after, she was promoted to store manager at one of the branches located close to her home and left Playdeck. I truly missed her, but her memory is always with me. During the last quarter of my university studies, my cousin, who was in real estate, asked if I could buy a mink for her that was on sale on the second floor. She had seen the ad in the newspaper and came in to see me at the store. I said yes, and then she handed me an envelope with cash to pay for it. I was in shock and asked her how she got this money. She said it was legal earnings and then told me what she did for a living. She was in Real Estate, the financing side, and she had already earned $50,000 by June. This happened in October; I was floored. She was doing mortgage loans, and I immediately thought, "How can I sign up for that?"

I was only taking one last class that was all I needed to graduate in December, the year of 1985. She generously told me what to do, and I followed every single step she told me. I took real estate courses alongside it, got my license in December, and also graduated that month. I started working part-time with my cousin, who taught me the ropes. I kept my part-time job at Bullock's for a year, but eventually, I was making such good money in real estate that I gave up my job at the store and my dream of becoming a buyer.

SYLVIA VILLASENOR

The switch to real estate offered better pay, stability, and a lifestyle more aligned with my goals. I wanted to get married and have children, and I realized that the life of a buyer, with all the travel and demands, wasn't for me. It was a major turning point, and that decision shaped my future.

When you are a kid, you think about a lot of things. You start weaving big dreams. You see celebrities on television and manifest a life like them. You want to become that person who has it all. But some dreams are meant to be shattered. You have to accept the harsh reality and adjust to what life has planned for you; whether you love it or hate it, you have to become friends with the things you come across and end up bonding as your career. Therefore, I enjoy working at the store, but I miss doing loans. I found a deep sense of compatibility in that job, to the point where I didn't even see it as just a job anymore, but I found a different kind of comfort and satisfaction in helping people get their financing and move them into new homes, especially the ones who have worked their fingers to the bone to save enough for their down payment and qualify for a mortgage loan. It was one of the happiest feelings of my life to be the person who handed them the keys to their new homes.

I believe that pursuing an education, like earning a degree, isn't just about the knowledge you gain—it's about grounding yourself in the discipline of completing something significant. Whether it takes four, five, or six years, it's the commitment to seeing it through those matters. For me, starting with an associate degree in merchandising was a steppingstone toward becoming a buyer for a department store. But I realized that wasn't enough. I felt the need to prepare myself further, so I transferred to the university to get my bachelor's degree in marketing, a field that's broad and adaptable to various career paths.

It took me five years to complete my degree because I was working 30 hours a week while going to school part-time. The experience taught me that the degree itself, regardless of the field, can mold you in ways you never expected. It wasn't about becoming a doctor, lawyer, or architect. My degree in marketing could lead me to any number of roles in sales, management, or other business areas. The value of the degree wasn't necessarily in the specific knowledge I gained but in the fact that I took the time to start something challenging and saw it through to the end.

Sometimes, employers don't even focus on your GPA; they look at your work experience and the fact that you completed your education. It demonstrates that you have the stability, determination, and resilience to begin something and finish it, no matter where that path eventually leads.

Back then, during the women's liberation movement, I remember a particular commercial that really stuck with me. It was a television commercial, and there was this woman in a business suit. The message was all about empowerment, but it also highlighted the pressure on women to do it all. The jingle went something like, *"I can bring home the bacon" (meaning money), "fry it up in a pan,"* and still, *"never forget you're a man."*

SYLVIA VILLASENOR

It was a catchy tune, but thinking back, it also reflected the exhausting expectations placed on women. We were expected to succeed professionally, take care of the household, and still maintain this ideal image of a supportive partner. That kind of pressure is really exhausting. It was a time of progress, but it also set incredibly high standards for women to live up to, which wasn't always realistic or fair.

The idea that you have to do it all can be overwhelming, but finding balance and being there for your kids is invaluable. It's okay not to be everything all at once—being present is what truly matters in the long run.

But then you realize, wow, you can achieve all that and still be a modern-era woman. I worked so hard that balancing my personal and professional life became impossible. My daughter still resents me to this day for not being around. Yet, I find peace in knowing that I've given my children a privileged life—a life many can only dream of but never attain. Had I not been there to provide for my children, they might have felt the pressure to work at a very young age, something I deeply wished to shield them from. I wanted them to savor their teenage years, free from the burdens of stepping into the adult world too soon—a world where earning a living can overshadow the fleeting magic of childhood. My hope was for them to experience the joy and freedom of youth without the weight of responsibilities too early.

MAMA'S PEARLS

Chapter 4
Trials and Tribulations

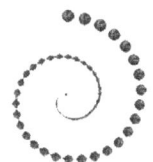

Some people can only see the glittering surface of your life from outside the window, admiring what seems like a perfect, privileged existence. But they will never know the backstage story—the unseen days and years of struggle, sacrifice, and pain that you have endured to reach this point of stability. What they witness is only the shine, never the shadows that came before. As Molière said, *"The greater the obstacle, the more glory in overcoming it."*

There is something about being thrown into the unknown, a kind of *baptism by fire*, that forces you to discover what you're truly made of. My transition to middle school was at age twelve. I was bused as part of an integration program to a new neighborhood, felt exactly like that—a test of strength, adaptability, and courage. It was not just about fitting into an unfamiliar environment; it was about finding out who I was when everything around me was unfamiliar. Things were emotionally challenging and shaped my perspective on life. The first day stepping off the bus, I felt like I had entered a different world. The neighborhood was different, the school was different, and even the air seemed lighter. I was not sure if it was the excitement of a new place or the sense of safety that surrounded me, but something about that middle-class neighborhood felt like a fresh start.

For the next three years, this place would be my home away from home. It was cleaner, friendlier, and had a sense of calm that was absent in my old neighborhood. The kids here did not see me as an outsider—they welcomed me like I belonged. Despite the differences in our backgrounds, we formed friendships that felt genuine from the very first day.

It was a strange feeling, standing in a place that didn't feel quite like mine, yet somehow felt safe. It made me reflect on where I came from and where I wanted to go. Here, in this new place, I wasn't just a kid being bused in from another part of town—I was part of something bigger, something kinder. For the first time in a long while, I could breathe easily.

Years earlier, when I was nine years old, moving from Kenmore Ave to 12th Street marked a meaningful change for me. On Kenmore, life felt light and fun. I still remember Jeannie, Tavo, Tavo's cousin Katie and her children, who lived just down the block. We spent countless days together, forming bonds that made that house feel like a true home. But everything shifted when we moved to 12th Street. That summer of 1968, when we returned from Mexico, we found ourselves in a new home—our own house, the one my father had bought. My oldest sister, Espe, had moved out with her husband, Jaime, and their new baby, Jaime Jr. She was only a block away, but her absence was palpable. Espe had been more than just a sister; she was my protector. Whenever my father's anger scared me, she was there, reassuring me that everything would be okay. Her presence had been a bandage over wounds I didn't fully understand at the time. But, at the age of nine—almost ten—I sensed that things were changing. It was as if they expected me to be more independent, to do more things on my own without relying on any one of them. And with Espe gone, I had to learn to face the world without that comforting shield by my side.

My sister Lupe, who was a year older than me, wanted to start dating at the age of 13, regardless of my father unapproving it. He approved dating at age 15, but my sister was aggressive, wanting to grow up fast and dress up like an adult at age 13. She wanted to wear pantyhose, even if they were torn. It was almost comical, but my older sisters let her be. On the other hand, I wanted to stay a child, and it left me feeling out of place. In a sense, isolated and lonely because Lupe's free time was now spent with her older friends doing things teenagers did. Sheila would invite her to parties on weekends, and Lupe fit in well. Meanwhile, I was left alone at home, which was an emotionally challenging time for me. And they did not seem to care. I was at an age where you are transitioning from childhood into something more, and yet no one was guiding me. Everyone was minding their own business, leaving me feeling like an outcast. When I tried to insert myself, I was met with, "What are you doing? Just find something to do. Have some friends over." But in a big city, it was not that easy. Unlike a small town, where friends lived nearby, here, everyone was far away, and getting to someone's house was not simple. I was terrified to be far from home unless I had a ride, and rides were not always available. It was a suppressed feeling, a sense of isolation I was not strong enough to handle.

I still wanted to be a kid, so I found comfort at Espe's house. I found myself gravitating more towards her new place. She needed me. She needed me to take care of the baby and help her cook, and I found purpose in that need. Spending those years with her, I picked up on her cooking skills. She was meticulous—everything had to be super neat and wrapped perfectly, with not a single hair or foreign object ending up in the food. Her attention to detail and cleanliness became something I absorbed, and it healed me in a way. It helped soothe the feelings of loneliness and displacement I had when we first moved to 12th Street. While everyone else seemed to be running around, escaping home after school or work, I felt like I had nowhere to go. Lupe always had her friends, but they were older girls, too old for me to fit in. So, I stayed with Espe, finding comfort and learning in her kitchen.

While I watched the baby, Espe cooked the meals she would sell during the week to her coworkers. She worked at a men's pants manufacturer downtown, a tall building with three or four stories. There were few food options nearby, so the owners let her sell her delicious homemade meals to the workers. Espe was an incredible cook, and she took orders throughout the week, spending weekends—and sometimes midweek—cooking. My job was simple: helping with small tasks and caring for the baby. It was there that I found my place, my niche. Espe would give me five dollars for a weekend's work or seven if I helped twice in one week. But I did not do it for the money. I wanted to be there. It was a refuge for me, a place where I felt needed and appreciated. If it got late, I could stay the night, which was exactly what I wanted—to stay away from the places where I didn't feel like I belonged. Being with Espe made me feel like I was where I was supposed to be, at least for the time being, and that made everything a little bit easier.

I felt that loneliness all over again when Ruth, Jeannie, Lupe, and Sheila got married, and Tony moved out to his own apartment. Suddenly, it was just Dad and me, the last two left at home. We had nothing in common. We barely spoke. He would sit down at the dinner table like always, and by then, I was the one cooking our meals. We would eat together because he liked that routine, but there wasn't much to say. I would come home from work or school to an empty house, and the silence was suffocating. It was just my dad and me, sitting across from each other, eating near silence, with nothing to discuss. After dinner, I would retreat to my room, the emptiness of the house pressing down on me. I would sit there and think, *this is ugly. Is this it?* I must have been around 15 when Lupe left—going on 16. That is such a critical age. You need support during those years because so much is changing, and your mind can feel like it's going through hell. I had a boyfriend at the time, but he was very possessive. Looking back, I laugh at my own silliness—how could I have ever given control of my life to someone else like that? He wouldn't let me go out with my friends or have a good time.

MAMA'S PEARLS

And everyone knew he was my boyfriend, so the other guys at school wouldn't even approach me. They were afraid to talk to me because they knew him. I found myself trapped in a situation that felt wrong. By this time, I was 17, and all I could think was, *What am I doing here?* I wasn't ready to get married. It was my first serious relationship, and I didn't want to jump into any life-altering decision. My dad thought, *Yeah, this is it. She'll get married as soon as she's done with high school.* But my boyfriend had dropped out of school. He didn't like to work, and I started suspecting he might have been involved in something illegal on the side—though I never knew for sure. He wasn't someone I could imagine building a life with, yet I felt trapped. I didn't know how to break free because I was afraid of what he might do if I tried to leave.

It wasn't love, really. It was fear. But at the beginning, I have to admit, it was something special. I was 14, not even 15 yet. It was that kind of innocent puppy love where neither of us had anything to offer the other except our time. You know, the kind of love that gives you butterflies in your stomach, only to realize later it wasn't worth the butterflies at all. We spent a lot of time together, and when I turned 15, I told him that if he wanted to come to my house, he'd have to ask my dad for permission. He asked, *"What do I do?"*

I said, *"Well, Dad's usually watering the plants on Sunday mornings around 10. You can stop by on your bike and talk to him in Spanish. Ask if we can be boyfriend and girlfriend."* A week after my 15th birthday, it happened. My dad was out there tending the lawn when my boyfriend rode up on his bike. In his broken

Spanish—because his parents were born here too—he said, *"Hey, Manuel, is it okay if Sylvia and I are boyfriend and girlfriend?"* My dad started laughing and called me over. *"But you just turned 15 last week!"* He said. It was all lighthearted and fun then—two kids enjoying each other's company. Maybe because I was so lonely, it seemed perfect, him on his bike, just being there for me. Once I had him behind me, I felt a sense of freedom I hadn't known before. I could finally focus on school, finish my studies, and continue working at Bullocks without that constant weight on my shoulders. But it was strange—his possessiveness didn't just end with the breakup. It lingered, even in my dreams. I would find myself running from him in my sleep, terrified that he was chasing me. It was almost like an obsession, as if it was either me or nothing in his mind. I don't know what you'd call it—maybe a "dream chaser"— but it haunted me. I couldn't shake the fear that if I stayed with him, one day, he might actually kill me, bury me in the backyard, and no one would ever know. It was a dark, ugly thought, and it terrified me. From then on, I never allowed myself to be in that situation again. I became much more careful about who I dated, always mindful of the warning signs.

I do remember the friction of a tense time when my sister Jeannie told me that when we first moved to Guadalajara after Mom passed away, Grandma Ruth, Dad's Mom, told them that I would be staying with her. I was five months old. No one liked it, and everyone was upset. They all wanted us to stay together as a family. My mom's side of the family, especially my grandma and my mom's youngest sister, Nina Jose, were angry about it, even though they picked me up daily to spend most of the afternoon with them, and the distance between the two houses was merely a four-minute walk. They all took it hard and were a bit bitter about the arrangement. I remember spending time with them and hearing their complaints about Grandma Ruth. It was little things, like how she combed my hair or how she dressed me. They were very particular about our appearances. Mom's family also made sure we looked impeccable and well-groomed.

My maternal grandma ran a side business selling fabric and clothing she bought from wholesale vendors to resell them at retail pricing for both adults and children. She would dress us in homemade dresses or clothing from her vendors. The dresses were short and trendy for girls our age. Grandma Ruth bought fabric and sewed all my dresses. But the dresses she would sew for me were much longer in length, a little above the knee. It made me look like a very modest 3, 4 and 5 year-old, as if she was prepping me to become a nun. Yes, my sister made a little fun of me.

They were also curious, wanting to know, "How's grandma Ruth treating you? You think she will mind if the dress we bought for you is too short?" But I was only a toddler—I didn't know how to answer. Somehow, whatever I said would get back to my grandma Ruth, and it would turn into a big issue at times. The small-town talk seemed to magnify everything. Both sides would be upset with me over things I didn't even understand. It was silly and uncomfortable, and I felt as if I was in the middle of a battle between the two households. This type of tension for a child was not necessary, and it lasted until we moved back to the States.

There were times that my older sisters thought I was too spoiled because I was with my dad's mom and believed she and the rest of the family spoiled me. But it wasn't like that. They were just a bit overprotective and were just trying to take care of me, just as my mom's side of the family was trying to do. In a sense, I was very fortunate to have been looked after by both Mom and Dad's side of the family. Up to this day, our cousins on Dad's side of the family, who were there from day one, see me as a sister. Now, I see that as a blessing in disguise.

When we moved to the States, that tension faded into the background, but new challenges emerged. At that time, my older sisters had the responsibility to look after us. They made sure we were clean and sent us to school in good shape.

My three older sisters had so much on their plate once we moved back to the States. They had the responsibility of looking after us from A through Z and some extra. I remember one time when I was in the 3rd grade, I volunteered to bring a wedding cake for our teacher. She was getting married, and we had a potluck bridal party for her. I do not know whose idea it was to include a wedding cake, but no one raised their hand to one. I felt bad, so I volunteered to bring it without consulting with my sisters first; it all happened so fast. I was nine years old and felt a jolt in my stomach when I was appointed to bring the wedding cake. When I went home, I told my sisters I needed them to bake me a wedding cake for my teacher. Their jaws dropped when I said for tomorrow!! Espe laughed so hard

MAMA'S PEARLS

Jeannie and Ruth looked furious. They drew names to see who was going to bake it, and Ruth, the 15-year-old at the time, lost. She was furious but baked the cake, burnt it and there was not enough white frosting to hide the burnt crust. I was so embarrassed to show up with it the next morning but I delivered, and none of the kids in my class had cake other than the adults there. The important thing was I delivered it at my sister Ruth's expense, and she let me have it. The responsible ones for us at home were frustrated with me and I guess I deserved it. I never pulled that trick again. After Dad scolded me, I felt so insecure, like nothing I did was ever right. I was constantly questioning myself, wondering how to get things right when no one was explaining anything to me. Instead, they would get mad, talk about it among themselves, and then ignore me for a while. Even when they helped me, they did so reluctantly, dragging themselves around, which only made me feel more uncomfortable and insecure about my surroundings. It made me feel like a burden.

When I went to school, I carried those feelings with me. I felt like I had to watch everything I said, afraid of making mistakes. My English wasn't very good, and the teacher, with 22 other kids to manage, seemed frustrated that she couldn't get through to me. It was such a hard time, and I don't even know how to explain how strange and out of place I felt.

At age 14, I had my first boyfriend, and I think I got so attached to him because he looked after me, took care of me, and made me feel wanted—something I had been craving for so long. Helping Espe at her house gave me a similar feeling of being needed, of having a place where I belonged. But there were also moments when the girls at home were sensitive and regretted how they treated me. They would try to make up for it, taking me out to eat or including me in family outings. They never truly left me behind, but it took time for them to get over their own frustrations. Sometimes, I think they were just exhausted from taking on so much responsibility. I imagine they must have thought, *Why don't I just get married and have my own kids instead of raising my dad's kids?*

It was a struggle, you know, and I think that's why having a boyfriend at such a young age was so appealing to me. He made me feel like I mattered, like I was important to someone. But eventually, that relationship soured, and when it ended, I found myself back in the same lonely place I had been before, only this time with more experience—both good and bad. It was like I had come full circle, but now, with the weight of those years and experiences on my shoulders.

When I started college, my life took a turn that I hadn't anticipated. For the longest time, I hadn't been in a serious relationship. There had been brief flings here and there, but nothing that truly stuck. I was 22 when my father retired and moved to our hometown in Guadalajara, Mexico. The dynamics at home shifted dramatically: my brother returned to the house, and Sheila, who had recently left her husband, joined us as well. It was the three of us living together, and I found that, as I grew older, the respect and camaraderie among us deepened. We got along much better than before.

MAMA'S PEARLS

One of the most significant changes was having a car. My dad had bought me a Dodge Demon—it was a white color car with a name that seemed almost ironic given its emblematic presence. With that car, my social life began to blossom. Friends suddenly appeared, eager to join me for outings. The car became a symbol of my newfound freedom and social status. I didn't mind that some were drawn to me because of the car. It was a small price to pay for the companionship and camaraderie that it brought.

I remember the thrill of driving around with my friends. There were times when we'd cram five to six girls into the car, laughing and chatting as we drove through town. It was a stark contrast to the loneliness I felt during my earlier years, where high school had often seemed like an endless stretch of dark tunnel with no light at the end. The struggle to balance my academic pursuits with my personal life left me feeling isolated at times.

The journey through university was grueling. It took me six years to complete my studies, culminating in a bachelor's degree by the time I was 25. During those years, I was single, navigating a series of casual relationships that never quite materialized into something meaningful. Despite my independence, there were many nights spent crying myself to sleep, feeling the weight of my solitude more acutely when I returned home.

Once Sheila remarried, it was just my brother and me in the house. Those empty feelings came back, the sense of isolation that was hard to articulate. It wasn't until after graduation, when I obtained my real estate license and finally purchased a new car, that

SYLVIA VILLASENOR

I felt a shift in my life. I moved out of the family home and into a studio apartment above Jeannie's garage. It was a new chapter where I felt more independent and in control in comparison to those transitional years when there were numerous nights of tears and misunderstandings. My sisters, entrenched in their own lives with their children and marital challenges, often viewed my independence with criticism rather than support. Their harsh judgments, at times, felt like a personal betrayal. They saw my freedom as if I were wasting the years away for marriage rather than celebrating my aspiration to obtain a higher education first. I tried to ignore it and instead supported them in any way I could. I helped Ruth with her children and took them out on weekends, treating them to movies and their favorite hamburgers from Tommy's—a local spot known for its enormous chili burgers.

The memory of those weekends and the joy I saw on their young faces remained a bright spot in my life. As they look back to those years, they also remember those times fondly. It was my way of connecting with them, offering a bit of joy, allowing me an escape from my demanding life. The effort was worth it, and it was a reminder that, despite the challenges and the loneliness, there were moments of connection and kindness that shaped my journey.

Little things like taking the kids out and treating them to Tommy's Burgers ended up being more appreciated by them than by their parents. My sisters, who had settled into their own lives and marriages at a young age, in my eyes seemed to regard my independence with a mix of confusion and a bit of criticism. To them, I was moving on a path they hadn't taken, one that diverged from the expected route of early marriage and family life.

I wasn't trying to appear arrogant; I was simply immersed in my own busy life. I stayed connected by helping them with their children to free their weekends when needed. They appreciated the help but struggled to understand my choices and the freedom I pursued. It was as if my own contentment and independence reflected their own unfulfilled dreams or regrets even though they were great housewives and mothers. The truth was, in my loneliness, I aspired to become like them one day.

Therefore, connecting with my nieces and nephews as we spent our time together was healing. Because I was so young when they were born, they never called me "Auntie"—instead, they addressed me by my first name. To a ten-year-old, "Auntie" felt too distant and formal, so my first-name basis with them felt more natural. Their presence and affection helped me find solace and a sense of purpose.

As I grew older, the question of when my own life would take a significant turn loomed large. My father was concerned, often expressing his worry that I might never marry. I would reassure him, though it felt like an elusive promise. But then, at 28, something changed. I had a friend at Cal State L.A. that I had known for five years. He began to pursue more than friendship after we graduated. It took me a while to accept his motive, from a platonic friendship to a full-blown serious relationship. After a few months, I gave in, and within a year, we got married when we were 29 and at 30, Joy was born our first child. It was a moment of profound fulfillment.

SYLVIA VILLASENOR

We have been married for 36 years now and raised 3 children; in addition to Joy, Steven and Dean came along. Now, they are grown adults and my biggest blessing.

Growing up without a mother had left its mark. The absence of that guiding, nurturing presence was deeply felt, especially in moments when I needed someone to mend not just the physical scrapes but the inner wounds that lingered and shaped my emotional landscape. I often wondered how I managed to get through those years, grappling with the lack of a maternal figure who could soothe the deeper, invisible pains.

Reflecting on my sisters' struggles, I see echoes of my own experiences. They might have felt similar gaps and challenges, yet they seldom spoke about them. It was a shared silence among us— a silence that perhaps hid our common vulnerabilities and unspoken pain.

In my quieter moments, I would think about my mother and wish she could be there for me. I longed for her presence, imagining scenarios where she could just take me somewhere and bring me back the next day, offering a simple but comforting routine. But that wasn't possible. I was left to navigate my own path, often feeling the weight of her absence more acutely in those moments of need.

Grandma's teachings had always been my anchor. She instilled in me the understanding that, while human relationships are fraught with complexities and occasional disappointments, divine love is unwavering. "I might turn on you sometimes," she'd say, "because I'm human, and you might make me angry or disrupt my peace. But

God will never turn on you. He must come first before anyone, and He's your true father in this sense." Her words were meant to be a foundation, a reminder to prioritize faith and resilience.

Despite her wisdom, life was still challenging. Grandma knew that I would face tough times, and she tried to prepare me as best as she could. We were often separated by circumstances, and I understood that her guidance was limited by what she could offer from afar. Life seemed to have its own plan for me, and while Grandma's lessons provided strength, I often wished my mother could have been around to share in those moments.

Did her absence make me stronger? Perhaps. I learned to rely on the principles she imparted and to find resilience in the face of adversity. Yet, the void left by my mother's absence was never fully filled. I still yearned for her presence and the comfort of a mother's love.

Sometimes, I find myself pondering a profound question: would I be the person I am today if my mother had been around? If she had been with me and my siblings from my sister's Lupe and my birth in Los Angeles, would our lives have taken a different path? Perhaps I would have been more connected to my dad, developing an emotional bond with him from infancy. Instead, life events separated us when I was only five months old, and my father's visits were not frequent. This distance created a gap in our relationship that I felt acutely as I grew older.

Growing up, I saw how my older sisters had a closer relationship with Dad, which seemed more natural to them. For us younger ones, the connection was more strained. We lacked the patience and familiarity that came more easily to the older siblings. I often wondered if my mother had been there, would she have bridged the gap between my father and us, especially if she had been as involved and attentive as I tried to be with my own children. If she had been around, perhaps I would have felt more secure and less burdened by the harsh feelings I sometimes had towards my father.

It's easy to speculate about how things might have been different, but the reality is that I was left to navigate my own path. When my sisters moved on, I felt abandoned. I struggled with the isolation, caught between a distant father who was preoccupied with work and a lack of close friends. My social life was limited, and I spent much of my time working and taking the bus, with few opportunities for the kind of social interactions that might have eased my loneliness.

Looking back, I realize that my upbringing was unconventional and challenging. But I know I'm not alone in this experience; many others have faced similar struggles. Speaking about it now, the emotions still burn within me, indicating that I need to address and refresh these feelings. It's a reminder of how far I've come and the progress I've made.

Today, I am grateful for the family I have. Despite the difficulties and differences, we come together for birthdays and family gatherings. As we all approach the later stages of our lives, it's a time to seek peace with the emotions and experiences that have shaped us. We each carry our own burdens, but in the end, we find solace in the fact that we have each other.

MAMA'S PEARLS

There's a belief that we choose the family we come to in this life, and perhaps I chose this particular journey with all its ups and downs. Despite the trials, I'm thankful for the many siblings I have and the support we offer one another. If I had to go through these challenges, I'm glad it was with a large family by my side rather than facing it alone. Reflecting on where I am now, I realize how often I held myself back out of fear and insecurity. If I had been more assertive and less intimidated by my own doubts, I might have opened more doors and seized more opportunities. I see now that sometimes it's better to act despite your fears than to let them paralyze you completely.

There were countless moments when fear held me back from pursuing things I was passionate about. I remember wanting to enroll in extra classes or participate in extracurricular activities, but the anxiety of having to leave for these events while it was dark, or the fear of taking the bus alone, kept me from stepping outside my comfort zone. These fears, while seemingly small, were significant obstacles that stopped me from advancing my education and exploring new avenues.

Had I been willing to face these fears and embrace the uncertainty, I might have gained confidence and finished my education sooner—or perhaps pursued it to an even higher level. My insecurities and the lack of encouragement from those around me made it hard to believe in my potential. As a result, I missed out on opportunities that could have contributed to my growth.

SYLVIA VILLASENOR

In retrospect, I often found myself resenting my own hesitation. The regret of not taking that extra step lingered, reminding me of what might have been. It's a painful realization that my fears held me back from achieving both small and significant goals.

But this self-reflection is also a learning experience. It's a reminder that while fear can be paralyzing, the act of moving forward—even when scared—can lead to growth and success. It's a lesson in courage and self-belief, one that I hope to carry forward as I continue to navigate life's challenges.

To you, my dear reader, I want to share a piece of advice from my own journey: don't be afraid. Don't let fear silence your questions or hold you back from seeking help. Whether it's asking a teacher for clarification, reaching out to colleagues, or confiding in a sibling if you don't have a mother, don't let the fear of judgment keep you from speaking up.

If you find yourself struggling to explain something, even if you're trembling or on the verge of tears, ask for a bit more time. It's worth the effort. People might surprise you with their understanding if you give them a chance to hear you out. Hiding away in silence only leads to misunderstandings and missed opportunities. Others may perceive your silence as a lack of effort or interest when, in reality, you're just struggling to find the right words.

Don't let age or perceived authority intimidate you. Even if someone is older or in a position of power, remember that your voice matters. If you're faced with a language barrier, for instance, don't let embarrassment prevent you from trying to communicate. It's far better to try to explain yourself, even if it feels uncomfortable, than to shy away out of fear of looking foolish.

I spent many years afraid to speak out, worried about making mistakes or being judged. This fear kept me from taking chances and exploring opportunities that might have been within my reach. Looking back, I realize that if I had been braver, if I had been willing to take that chance and open doors that seemed out of my reach, I might have achieved even more.

So, my advice is simple: do it scared. It's okay to feel nervous or uncertain. It's better to take that step than to let fear hold you back, even if you feel like you might make a mistake. You never know how others will respond to your effort to communicate. Sometimes, it's the courage to speak up and reach out that can make all the difference.

Throughout my journey, there have been moments when the weight of emotional turmoil felt unbearable, and I desperately needed a sanctuary to recharge and find strength. For me, that sanctuary was always my grandmother's home in Guadalajara.

During my years in school or at work, when the pressures felt overwhelming, I would retreat to this place of refuge. My grandma's house, with its warm embrace and the presence of my cousins and aunts, became my haven. I would travel there every summer, arriving in late June and staying until mid-September. Those months spent with my family in Guadalajara were a lifeline, a time when I felt enveloped by love and affection.

SYLVIA VILLASENOR

Returning to that familiar place provided a profound sense of renewal. Each visit was like a deep breath of fresh air, recharging my spirit and making me feel invincible. The support and warmth from my family made me believe that no challenge was too great. When it was time to leave and return to my daily life, I felt fortified by the strength and love I had received during those summer months.

But after three months of my return, by December, I found myself back in my regular routine; the comfort of my grandmother's home seemed a world away. The transition back could be jarring, and the strength I had felt during those months sometimes seemed to fade by Christmas. I missed the security of having a place to run to, where I could find solace in my grandma's presence.

I remember how, as a child, I would curl up in the folds of her long cotton skirts, finding a small, comforting space to bury my head. She would soothe me with gentle words and tender touches, reminding me that everything would be alright. The reassurance she provided was a balm for my anxieties, a temporary escape from the pressures of life.

My dad's half-sister, Nina Chila, who also experienced the loss of her mother at a young age, offered similar comfort. Her understanding and empathy helped bridge the gap left by my grandmother's absence. Together, they created a cocoon of support that made difficult times more bearable.

If you find yourself struggling with emotional challenges, I encourage you to seek out your own sanctuary, a place or space where you can recharge and feel reassured. Whether it's a physical location, a person, or a specific activity, having a refuge can make a significant difference. It's these moments of reprieve that can provide the strength to face the world anew, ready to tackle the challenges ahead.

The warmth and support I received from my grandmother and my aunt were profound and rooted in their own experiences of loss and struggle. My grandmother, who had lost her own mother at a young age, and my aunt, who was also mourning the absence of her mother, understood my pain in a way that few others could. Their empathy and kindness created a nurturing environment where I felt truly cherished.

Their love was the most valuable gift they could offer—an unspoken understanding that went beyond material things. Whether it was a shared meal or simply their comforting presence, their support was a balm for my troubled spirit. Their encouragement and the affection they showered upon me helped to build a shield of resilience, allowing me to face life's challenges with renewed strength.

On the other hand, my mom's side of the family provided a different kind of solace. Nina Jose, with her unwavering support and fierce determination, was a constant reminder of my own worth. Her encouragement to rise above adversity and not let others bring me down was a source of strength that carried me through difficult times.

These three months spent with my extended family were healing, offering a reprieve from the struggles I faced back in the States.

They provided a sense of belonging and reassurance that I carried with me as I returned to my daily life, ready to confront whatever lay ahead.

If you have a person or a place that offers you similar support— a sanctuary where you feel understood and valued—cherish it. Such spaces are invaluable, providing the strength and reassurance needed to navigate life's challenges. For me, those summer months in Guadalajara with my loving family were more than just a retreat; they were a crucial part of my journey, helping me to move forward with hope and resilience.

At 22, I turned to the Christian faith for support during challenging times. I found solace and guidance in prayer and the Bible, sensing that God was watching over me and guiding my path. This spiritual connection became crucial in my life, as I wanted to avoid repeating past mistakes and relying on relationships that didn't serve me well. I had to be strong and self-reliant, both personally and spiritually, rather than depending on others to make me feel whole.

I recognized the difficulty in waiting for the right opportunities and the challenges of sticking to my faith, especially when mistakes were made. Despite the trials, I have leaned on God rather than human relationships to navigate life's ups and downs.

The title "Mama's Pearls" holds deep significance for me because it reflects how my mother viewed her seven children. Despite her sudden and unexpected death, she knew three days before passing that she would be leaving us behind. She saw each of us as her precious pearls, part of a treasured necklace. With six daughters and one son, I imagined the pearls as representing us—beige pearls for the girls and a unique light gray pearl for our brother. The book explores what became of her pearls—how we lived and coped after she was gone.

The memoir delves into life after her departure, the experiences we faced without her, and the impact of my father's role in our lives. Although my father carried much of the burden, I wanted to honor the woman my mother was, reflecting on how I might have felt in her place. The book also highlights the wisdom and qualities she embodied, which I strive to incorporate into my own life. Despite my father's advice to avoid having many children—something he said could strain a marriage—I understand the challenges my mother faced and the remarkable strength she displayed in raising us.

Chapter 5
Moments of Connection

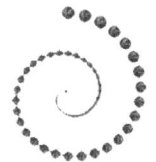

"A mother is not a person to lean on, but a person to make leaning unnecessary."

Dorothy Canfield Fisher.

Mothers have a way of shaping their children that's so subtle we often don't recognize it until much later in life. It's not always about the big, obvious moments. Sometimes, it's about the small, everyday things they do, the quiet strength they show, and the lessons they teach without ever saying a word. A mother's love runs deep, but so does her determination to help her child grow into someone who can stand tall on their own.

Think about it—mothers are there to hold us when we're young, to guide us when we're unsure, and, eventually, to let us go so we can find our own way. That's the beauty of the relationship. It evolves. As children, we might rely on them for everything, but as we grow older, we realize their true gift is teaching us how to rely on ourselves.

It's the same for every daughter. We grow up seeing our mothers as our safety net, our home base. But as we step into adulthood, we come to understand that their greatest act of love is giving us the tools to be independent to navigate life's highs and lows on our own terms.

Though my mother passed away when I was only four months old, her presence lingered with me in ways I couldn't always explain. As I grew older, there were countless moments when I yearned for her—times when I needed her guidance, her warmth, and the comfort that only a mother could provide. But in her absence, I learned to connect with her through other means, and it was in those quiet moments of reflection and longing that I felt her most.

Growing up in a household where all my sisters had moved on, and it was just my father and me, there were many lonely days. My father, though kind, wasn't the emotional type, and I often found myself retreating to my room after a hard day. It was during these times that I would close my eyes and imagine my mother there, sitting beside me, her hand resting gently on my shoulder. I didn't have memories of her to fall back on, but I had something just as powerful: the idea of her.

In many ways, her absence shaped my understanding of motherhood. I saw my friends with their mothers, and I observed the small yet meaningful ways they interacted—how their mothers would pack their lunches, bring them new clothes for school, or show up to school events. I watched with a mixture of envy and curiosity, wondering what that bond felt like. Would my mother have been like theirs? Would she have been the one cheering me on at my school plays or helping me prepare for my exams?

One of the hardest moments I remember happened during school. It was Mother's Day, and there was a special event where students were invited to perform—poems, short recitals, and little performances meant to celebrate the bond between mothers and their children. I stood backstage, nervous, gripping the small sheet of paper with the words to my poem. I remember glancing around at my classmates, most of them buzzing with excitement. Some were smiling, looking out into the audience where their mothers sat proudly, waving at them.

But I had no one to wave at. My mother wasn't there—she never would be. I knew that from the moment the event was announced but knowing didn't make it any easier. It didn't stop the ache in my chest or the lump in my throat.

It came time for me to step up to read my poem. As I walked onto the stage, I looked out at the sea of faces in the audience, searching for someone who wasn't there. There were mothers scattered everywhere, smiling and holding up cameras, capturing the moments they'd cherish forever. But in the sea of proud parents, all I saw was an empty chair. It was as if that one chair represented all the absence I felt in my heart. And for a second, I pretended she was there, sitting in that very spot, smiling at me, listening to my words like she had never left. I imagined her applauding after I was done, telling me how proud she was, and giving me a hug.

But when the clapping started and I looked back at the empty chair, reality hit me all over again. She wasn't there, and she never would be. The hardest part wasn't just knowing that she couldn't be with me—it was feeling the weight of that absence every time I had a moment that needed celebrating, every time I needed her support.

As a kid, it was hard to explain that kind of emptiness. How do you tell someone you're looking at a crowd full of smiling faces, but you feel lonelier than ever? How do you explain what it's like to search for someone who won't ever show up? I couldn't. So I didn't. I just held on to the image of her in my mind as if pretending was enough to fill the void, even if just for a second.

That was one of the moments that taught me about resilience. When you grow up without a mother, you learn how to find strength in places where it might not naturally exist. You learn to imagine the encouragement that others can take for granted. It was in those empty chairs and silent moments that I began to realize I had to be strong for myself.

When I was younger, I didn't know how to process that absence. The feeling of missing someone I had never truly known was complex, confusing even. I knew of her from stories, from fragments of memories shared by my older sisters, but I didn't have my own memories to hold on to. And yet, I felt her absence deeply. It wasn't just about not having a mother—it was about not having that anchor, that figure who is supposed to guide you through the challenges of growing up, the person who helps you make sense of the world.

In my quiet moments, I found myself imagining what it would have been like if she had been there. When I came home after a hard day at school, I imagined her welcoming me, her arms open and ready to hold me as I vented my frustrations. When my friends told stories about their mothers teaching them how to cook or guiding them through teenage heartbreaks, I would picture my mother sitting beside me, offering me advice. These thoughts weren't based on any specific memory or reality, but they were a way for me to connect with her, even in her absence.

And at times in life the absence of someone can feel just as powerful as their presence. For me, my mother's absence became something I carried with me every day, shaping me in ways I didn't fully understand until much later in life. Even though she wasn't physically there, the longing for her, the what-ifs, and the small glimpses of what motherhood should have been for me influenced the way I saw the world around me. And while she wasn't there to hold my hand, there were moments when other women stepped in— unintentionally but beautifully—to fill those gaps.

One of those women was Mom's sister, Nina José. She married late in life, well into her forties, which was unusual at the time. She had no children of her own, but she became like a second mother to me and my siblings. Looking back, I realize how much she took on that role without even thinking about it. She was always there for us, especially during those difficult times when we needed a mother figure. I would often watch her move around the house, doing things

MAMA'S PEARLS

I imagined my mother might have done.

Nina José had a warmth about her, but it was her quiet strength that always stood out to me. She was fiercely independent, much like how I imagined my mother would have been. Even though she never had children of her own, she mothered us all in her own way. I sometimes thought about how she learned that from her own mother and my mom. My grandma and my mother were the two women who had shaped her into the strong, nurturing figure she became.

She never bore a full-term pregnancy, though she tried a few times. So, we were her babies. All seven of us. She poured all her love into us, and I often wondered if she modeled that care after my mother. Every time she came to visit, the house would light up. She'd cook us delicious meals, make sure we had enough clothes and shoes, and always find a way to make us laugh. It was as if she had this endless reservoir of love to give, and she never held back.

I used to think, when I was about ten or eleven, that if my mother were still with us, she'd be just like Nina José—loving, warm, strong, and always making sure we had everything we needed. In many ways, my aunt became the mother I longed for, filling that void in my heart, even though she was modeling on someone she herself had lost.

And then there was my friend Gina I met her when I was twelve, and we quickly became inseparable. Spending time with her and her family opened my eyes to the kind of mother-daughter bond I'd only ever dreamed of. Her mother and father were loving, attentive, and always involved in her life. It was through them that I truly saw the "missing link" in my own life—the way a mother ensured her children had everything they needed, from food to clothes to emotional support.

It wasn't just the big things; it was the small details that stood out to me. The way her mom would take her shopping if there was a sale or just spend time with her on weekends, buying her new outfits or simply being there for her.

I couldn't help but feel jealous sometimes. Not in a mean way, but in that quiet, longing way that creeps in when you see someone have what you've always wanted. I would sit on the school bus with Gina, listening as she excitedly told me about what her mom had gotten her or where they were going that weekend. I would nod along, smiling, but inside, I felt that ache—knowing I'd never have those kinds of moments with my mother.

At home, things were different. We were a big family, and there were so many of us. We didn't have the luxury of new clothes every season or lunches packed with love. We had to make do with what we had. I had six or seven outfits for the entire school year, and I had to take care of them because I wasn't getting any more. That was just how it was. But seeing the contrast between my life and Gina's made me realize just how much I was missing.

Whenever I visited Gina at her house, her mom, Gladys, welcomed me in a warm way. She knew my story, and she was always kind to me. It felt like, for those moments, I got to borrow a little piece of what it was like to have a mother. Her mom passed away six years ago, and I still hold her with best regards. Through Gina's mom, I caught a glimpse of what motherhood was supposed to be. I saw the love, the care, the way a mother was supposed to cheer you on when things got tough. And I'd imagine that my mother would have done all those things for me, too. But instead, I found myself sitting with that feeling, that longing for something I couldn't quite grasp.

Those experiences shaped me, though. They taught me what I missed out on, but they also showed me what was possible. It wasn't always easy to accept, and sometimes the longing would overwhelm me. But I was lucky enough to have Nina José, who gave me a taste of the love and care I longed for.

And while no one could ever replace my mother, the women in charge of looking after me filled the empty spaces in my heart, even if just for a little while. I found fragments of what I had been missing – a comforting hand, a watchful eye, and a reassuring word. Yet, no matter how much they gave, the longing for my mother never fully went away.

As a child, it was easier to fill that gap with imagination. But as I grew older, especially in my teenage years, the longing became sharper, more real. I started to realize what I had been missing all along.

I remember one evening in particular. I was seventeen, feeling more alone than ever. I had come home after a day that had pushed me to my limits. I was used to it by then, the way the weight of the world seemed to sit squarely on my shoulders, but that day, it felt unbearable. The house was unusually quiet; no sounds of chatter, no footsteps in the hallway, just the hollow echo of my own thoughts bouncing around in my mind.

I locked myself in my room, lying on my bed, staring at the ceiling as if it held the answers to all the questions I didn't even know how to ask. The weight of the silence was deafening. It was one of those moments where I wished, more than anything, that I could have just one conversation with my mother, to hear her voice say, "Everything will be alright." But she wasn't there, and the ache of that absence felt deeper than ever.

My friends always talked about their mothers. They'd share stories about how their moms were there to comfort them after a hard day, offering advice, wiping away their tears, or just sitting with them, listening. I would listen to them, nodding along, pretending I knew what that kind of comfort felt like. But I didn't. Not in the way they did. I'd never had the luxury of running into my mother's arms when life felt too big, too hard. And in moments like that evening, I felt the emptiness of her absence more than ever.

As I lay there, I let myself imagine what it might have been like if she were there. What would she say? How would her presence change the way I felt at that moment? Would she know exactly what to say to ease my pain, to make the loneliness feel a little less suffocating? I imagined her sitting beside me, placing her hand gently on my shoulder, her voice calm and reassuring. I let myself believe, for just a moment, that she was there with me, that she could somehow hear the thoughts I couldn't put into words. And then, something happened. A warmth spread through me. It wasn't just a fleeting feeling—it felt real, tangible, as if someone had wrapped their arms around me, holding me close. My breath caught in my throat, and I closed my eyes, letting myself sink into that warmth, into the comfort of it. I didn't question it; I didn't try to explain it away. For the first time in what felt like forever, I allowed myself to believe that maybe, just maybe, my mother was there with me.

That warmth calmed the chaos inside my mind. The racing thoughts, the overwhelming emotions—they all began to fade, replaced by a stillness I hadn't felt in years. I lay there, wrapped in that sensation, and for the first time in a long while, I didn't feel so alone. I let myself hold onto the idea that my mother was there, watching over me, even if only in spirit. It wasn't something I could see or touch, but I felt it, and that was enough.

I didn't fight the feeling. Instead, I let it wash over me, filling the empty spaces inside of me. The tension I had been holding onto slowly unraveled, and I felt my body relax into the mattress. My mind, which had been running a mile a minute, finally quieted. And in that quiet, I found a kind of peace that I hadn't known I needed.

That night, for the first time in what felt like forever, I drifted into sleep easily, without the usual weight of worry pressing down on me. It wasn't a restless sleep filled with tossing and turning but a deep, peaceful slumber that carried me through the night. When I woke up the next morning, the warmth was gone, but the memory of it stayed with me. It reminded me that, even in her absence, my mother was still a part of me. And that thought—however fleeting—

was enough to carry me through the harder days that would follow.

These moments, though fleeting, were my way of connecting with my mother. They weren't built on memories or shared experiences but on a deep, emotional need that transcended time and physical presence. I often wondered how different my life might have been if she had been there for those moments, if I could have shared my thoughts with her if she could have offered me the comfort I so desperately craved.

As I hit adolescence, the need for my mother became more pronounced. My older sisters had been my support system, taking on a motherly role when I was younger, but with them gone living their own lives, I often found myself retreating into my own world.

My sisters had been fortunate enough to spend more time with her, and through their memories, I was able to paint a picture of the woman she had been. My mother had been a strong, independent woman, a hard worker. She was meticulous in everything she did, from the way she cooked to the way she raised her children. My sisters spoke of her with admiration, and I clung to their stories, piecing together the mother I never had the chance to know.

One of the things that stood out the most was how hardworking she was. Every morning, long before the sun rose, my mother was already tying her apron, her hands already busy in the butcher shop. By afternoon, she traded her knives for the machinery of the cotton company, her eyes heavy with fatigue but her determination unwavering. She did all of this while raising a house full of children. It wasn't easy, but she did it with grace and strength. Hearing these stories, I couldn't help but feel a sense of pride. My mother had been a remarkable woman, and even though I hadn't had the chance to experience her love and care firsthand, I felt her influence in my life.

It was through those stories that I began to understand the legacy she had left behind. She may not have been physically present in my life, but her values, her strength, and her love were passed down to me through my sisters. They had learned from her, and in turn, they had passed those lessons on to me. In many ways, my mother's absence taught me the value of resilience, independence, and finding strength in difficult circumstances.

As I reflect on my relationship with my mother—or rather, the absence of that relationship—I realize that her presence, though indirect, shaped me in profound ways. I learned to navigate life without her, but in doing so, I also learned how to connect with her in my own way; whether it was through the stories my sisters shared, or the quiet moments where I felt her presence, I found ways to keep her memory alive.

As much as I longed for her, I had to accept that my connection to my mother would never be like that of my friends or even my sisters. Their relationships with their mothers were built on shared moments, conversations, and memories—mine was built on imagination, on piecing together fragments from others. It was a difficult realization, but it also made me appreciate the women who were present in my life. My sisters, in their own ways, became maternal figures to me. They had known my mother in a way I never could, and through them, I caught glimpses of who she had been.

SYLVIA VILLASENOR

There was a particular day I remember vividly. It was during one of those difficult times in my teenage years when I felt especially lost and disconnected. I was sitting with one of my older sisters, and she began telling me a story about our mother. I had heard many stories over the years, but this one felt different. My sister spoke about how our mother would spend hours in the kitchen, carefully preparing meals for the family. She was meticulous about her cooking, making sure everything was perfect, even though she had so many other responsibilities. As my sister described the way our mother moved around the kitchen, I could almost see her there, apron tied around her waist, stirring a pot on the stove. It was in those moments, as I listened to my sister's voice, that I felt closest to my mother.

I realized that my mother's love and care were still present, even though she wasn't. They lived on in the way my sisters raised their own children, in the way they taught me to be independent and strong. I often imagined what it would have been like to cook with her, to learn from her directly, but I had to be content with what I had—her lessons passed down to me through the women she had influenced.

One particular story about my mother has stayed with me, though it came to me secondhand through my sisters. When my mother moved to the States, she found a way to help provide for her family by making and selling tamales. She would make dozens of them—ten or more—and sell them to friends, neighbors, and the local mom-and-pop stores. The shop owners got to know her, and they loved her cooking. In that small way, she built a reputation for herself, creating a business from her skill. My sisters would tell me how my mother was always working, always thinking of ways to help support the family, even when the world around her had changed so dramatically.

What's even more remarkable is what Dad found after she passed. When my father was cleaning out her side of the closet, he discovered one of his old hats filled with money—money my mother had saved from selling tamales. She had been saving it to visit her mother in Guadalajara. I remember hearing that story and feeling a surge of pride and sadness all at once. My mother had been resourceful, hardworking, and determined to stay connected to her roots, even while building a life in a new place. It made me wonder what other stories about her I'd never know, what other small acts of love and resilience she had shown that were lost to time.

One of the most powerful realizations I had as I grew older was that motherhood isn't always about direct interactions. It's about the legacy you leave behind, the values you pass on, even if you aren't there to see them take root. My mother's legacy lived on in all of us, in the way we cared for one another and in the strength we displayed in the face of adversity. I learned that being a mother isn't just about being physically present—it's about the impact you have and the love you leave behind.

Later in life, when I became a mother myself, I finally understood the full extent of what my mother must have gone through. The sleepless nights, the endless worries, the constant juggling of responsibilities—motherhood was far more demanding than I had ever imagined. And yet, it was also the most rewarding experience of my life. Holding my children in my arms, I felt a deep connection with my mother, a connection that transcended time and space. I knew that in those moments, she was with me, guiding me, even though she wasn't physically present.

Motherhood is about more than just providing for your children. It's about being there for them emotionally, about offering them a sense of security and love that they can carry with them throughout their lives. It's about passing down values, lessons, and traditions that shape who they become. And in that sense, my mother had been with me all along. She had passed down her strength, her resilience, and her work ethic through my sisters, and now it was my turn to pass those qualities on to my children.

There were times, of course, when I wished I could ask my mother how she had done it all—how she had managed to raise so many children while working multiple jobs, how she had found the strength to keep going when things got tough. But in the absence of her advice, I found my own way. I relied on the example she had set, even if I had never witnessed it firsthand. And in doing so, I realized that the most important thing she had given me was not her presence but her legacy.

I realized just how much my own experiences, both with and without her, would influence the way I raised my children. I wanted to give them the love and guidance I had missed out on, to be there for them in the ways my mother hadn't been able to be there for me.

But I also knew that my mother's strength was something I wanted to pass down to them.

In a way, my journey as a mother became a continuation of my connection to her. I found myself thinking of her often, especially in the early days of motherhood when everything felt new and overwhelming. There were moments when I wished she were there to offer advice or simply to reassure me that I was doing okay. But even in her absence, I felt her presence. I knew that the strength she had passed down to my sisters had been passed down to me, and now it was my turn to pass it down to my own children.

The years passed, and life continued to move forward, as it always does. I went to college, started my career, and built a life for myself, but there were always those moments when I would think of her. I often wondered how different things would have been if she had been there to witness those milestones. Would she have been proud of the person I had become? Would she have guided me through the difficult decisions, the heartbreaks, and the triumphs? These were questions that I knew I would never have answers to, but they lingered nonetheless.

You know, I often tell my sisters—even though I'm the youngest—that if I end up going first, they should be happy for me. Because then, I'll get to spend more time with our mom before they do. They already had their time with her, but I never got that chance. But now that I have granddaughters of my own, and as I hold them in my arms, I realize that, through them, I've come full circle. The love I missed from my mother, I can now give. And it's in those moments—when I see their little hands reaching for me—that I feel my mother's presence more than ever. Maybe she never left after all. Therefore, I will stay here on earth until the God Lord says otherwise.

MAMA'S PEARLS

Chapter 6
Reflecting on Growth

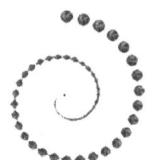

Looking back over my life, I've come to realize that each challenge I faced and each hurdle I crossed shaped me into the person I am today. There's no denying that life threw its fair share of obstacles my way, but the greatest realization was that I didn't have anyone to rely on but myself. No one was going to hold my hand or make the tough decisions for me. It was either I did it or I didn't. The fear of failure often lurked in the background, but eventually, I realized that not trying was far worse than any potential failure.

When I compare my experiences with those of people who had both parents supporting them and making choices for them, I see the stark difference in our lives. They didn't have to worry about falling or failing because they had a safety net. I didn't. Whatever I was going to achieve, I had to make it happen on my own. There was no waiting for the next opportunity to present itself; if something came my way, I had to sieve it. Sometimes, I wasn't sure if it was the right opportunity or not, but I knew I couldn't afford to be passive.

I remember applying for job after job, facing rejection after rejection. After the third or fourth interview with no success, doubt began to creep in. *What if I wasn't good enough? What if no one saw my potential?* But deep down, I knew I had to keep going. I couldn't let those rejections define me. I had to believe that the right opportunity was still out there, waiting for me to find it. And eventually, it did come. I landed a job that was a perfect fit for me. The waiting and the rejection were difficult, but when the right door opened, everything fell into place. Sometimes, you just have to keep pushing forward, trusting that the setbacks are leading you toward something better.

There were also times when I had multiple job offers and made the wrong choice. I remember one instance when I was offered two positions. One seemed secure, the other risky. I chose the secure one, only to regret it later. It wasn't fulfilling, and I realized that playing it safe doesn't always lead to satisfaction. Even though I had regrets, I took those experiences as lessons. It taught me that risks are worth taking and that even if things don't work out, it's better to try than to live with "what if."

In my personal life, I learned the importance of overcoming emotional hurdles and how they shaped my approach to relationships and decision-making. When I was younger, I often found myself looking for validation from others. I wanted to hear people tell me that I was on the right track and that I was doing the right thing. But as I grew older, I realized that not everyone's opinion mattered. Some people doubted me—not because they truly believed I would fail, but because they projected their own fears onto me. I had to stop letting their doubts influence my decisions.

One of the pivotal moments in my life came when I decided to continue my education after high school, a decision that would forever alter the trajectory of my future. It wasn't just about attending college – it was about stepping out of the mold that had been set for me by my family and society. My father wasn't supportive of this choice. To him, college seemed unnecessary, a distraction from the life he thought I should lead. He had seen my sisters marry young and settle into family life, and they seemed to be doing just fine without any higher education. He didn't see why my path should be any different. In his eyes, I should follow in their footsteps, get married, and move on with my life.

But I didn't want that for myself – not yet. I had more to accomplish and more to learn before settling down. I was determined to build a life that went beyond what was expected of me. This decision, however, clashed with my father's plans, plans that went far beyond just his hopes for me. You see, at that time, my father was also preparing to move forward with his own life. He was involved in a serious relationship with a woman who had children of her own, and they were planning to move in together. As the youngest child still at home, I knew that my decision to stay and attend college complicated things for him. It wasn't that he didn't care about my future – he did – but he saw things differently. In his mind, a college degree wasn't a guaranteed path to success, and he worried that it would only delay my ability to settle into a stable life. He was a practical man, and from his perspective, the sooner I could find my footing, the better off I would be.

I, on the other hand, felt that education was the key to unlocking a different kind of future, one where I could have more choices and control over my life. I didn't want to rush into marriage and family life without first exploring my own potential. But expressing this to my father wasn't easy. I could see the conflict in him—on one hand, he wanted what he thought was best for me, but on the other, he was grappling with how to balance his own plans and desires with mine.

Our conversations were difficult, and at times, I felt alone in my decision. I wasn't rejecting the life my father wanted for me, but I needed him to understand that my path might look different from the one he had envisioned. The tension between us wasn't born out of any lack of love or care—rather, it came from our different perspectives on what success and happiness looked like. He wanted me to be secure and settled, while I wanted the chance to pursue something more, even if it meant taking risks.

In the midst of this struggle, I turned to my grandmother for support. She had always been my confidante, the person I could rely on to understand me without judgment. I wrote her a letter, pouring out my feelings—how torn I felt between following my own dreams and meeting my father's expectations. I explained the situation, my desire to go to college, and how I feared I was standing in the way of my father's new life.

SYLVIA VILLASENOR

I mailed that letter, hoping for a response that would comfort me. But when the letter came, it wasn't addressed to me. Instead, my grandmother had written directly to my father. In her letter, she didn't mince words. She reminded him of the promises he had made to his daughters, of the responsibility he had to support us in our dreams and pursuits. She spoke of how he had always wanted the best for us and how denying me the opportunity to go to college would be a betrayal of those values. Her words were powerful, and they struck a chord with him in a way that my own words hadn't.

It wasn't long before my father came to me, letter in hand, a different expression on his face. He was still upset, but there was something else—something softer. He had read my grandmother's words, and they had made him rethink his position. He didn't apologize outright, but I could tell that he was beginning to understand. He relented, allowing me to stay in the house and pursue my education. It was a small victory, but for me, it felt monumental. I had stood up for what I wanted, and I had won. This wasn't just a win for me—it was a win for every young woman who had ever been told that her dreams weren't important, that her value lay in fulfilling someone else's expectations.

That moment marked a turning point in my life. It was the first time I truly fought for something I believed in, and it gave me the courage to keep fighting for what I wanted, even when others didn't understand. My father's reluctance wasn't born out of malice—he simply couldn't see beyond the traditional roles that society had set for women. But I could. And once I realized that I didn't have to conform to those expectations, my whole world opened up. College was my first step toward a future that was mine to define, and it wouldn't have been possible without my grandmother's intervention.

The journey wasn't easy—there were financial struggles, long nights of studying, and moments of doubt—but I knew that I was on the right path. I had chosen this path for myself, and that made all the difference. It wasn't just about the education; it was about proving to myself that I was capable of more than anyone had ever expected. It was about breaking free from the limitations that others had tried to impose on me. That decision to go to college was the first time I truly stepped into my own power, and it set the stage for everything that came after.

In the years that followed, I often thought back to that conversation with my father, to the letter from my grandmother that had changed everything. It reminded me that we all need someone in our corner, someone who believes in us when the world doesn't.

When I made the decision to go to college, I knew that the road ahead wouldn't be easy. I didn't have the luxury of simply applying and waiting for everything to fall into place. The reality of my situation was much more complicated. I didn't know how I was going to pay for it. Financially, it seemed impossible, and I wasn't even sure I had the grades to get into a decent school. Everything felt so overwhelming, like a tangled mess of worries in my mind. The idea of college was there, clear as day, but the steps to get there seemed murky at best.

SYLVIA VILLASENOR

At the time, I was working part-time and finishing high school. My job barely provided enough to cover my day-to-day expenses, let alone a college education. I wasn't sure where to even begin. Would I need loans? Could I even qualify for scholarships? How would I balance work and school? The more I thought about it, the more daunting it seemed. It was as if my dream of higher education was slipping through my fingers before I even had a chance to try.

And then there were my grades. They weren't terrible, but they certainly weren't exceptional. The competitive edge that many of my classmates had, the straight-A students destined for prestigious universities, wasn't something I could boast about. I felt like my academic record wouldn't open any doors for me. But despite all of that, I couldn't shake the feeling that college was where I needed to be. There had to be a way, even if I couldn't see it just yet.

One day, while researching options and talking to school counselors, I learned about something that would change everything: the Equal Opportunity Program (EOP). The program was designed to help students like me—students from minority backgrounds who didn't have the highest GPAs but who showed potential and a drive to succeed. As a Hispanic minority, I qualified for the program, and even though my GPA wasn't the impressive 3.5 that many scholarships required, it was high enough to meet the EOP's threshold. As long as my GPA was above 2.5, I had a shot.

When I found out that I qualified, it felt like the clouds had parted. It was the first glimpse of hope I'd had in weeks. The EOP provided financial aid, which would cover not only my tuition but also my books. For someone in my position, that was a game-changer. But the best part was that after all my tuition and book expenses were covered, I still had a little leftover—$140, to be exact. That money wasn't just spare change; it was the difference between me keeping my car and losing it. It covered my car payment, ensuring that I could still get to work, school, and anywhere else I needed to be. I couldn't believe my luck.

Suddenly, the overwhelming mess of worries in my head began to clear. Things were starting to make sense, and for the first time, I saw a path forward. The financial burden that had been weighing so heavily on my mind was no longer an obstacle. It wasn't easy by any means—I still had to juggle work and school, and I knew the road ahead would be long—but the door to college was finally open, and I was ready to walk through it.

With the financial aid secured and the support of the EOP, I threw myself into my studies. Even though it took me five years to complete my degree, I never gave up. I worked hard, balancing my part-time job with my coursework, pushing myself to keep going, even when it felt like too much. There were late nights and early mornings, days when I doubted myself, and moments when I wasn't sure I'd make it to the finish line. I often wondered what I was doing and whether I was capable of getting where I wanted to be. Living in the same house I grew up in, I remember thinking, *I need to move out of here. This isn't where I want to raise a family.* There were moments when I was ready to quit, to just give up and let someone else take care of me. I was tired—tired of trying so hard with no clear end in sight.

On top of that, there were people around me who doubted me too. A close friend of mine once told me that she didn't think I'd ever finish college. It hurt to hear that, but instead of letting her words defeat me, I used them as fuel to keep going. I realized that sometimes, the people who doubt us can be just as important in our journey as those who support us. Their doubt becomes a motivator, pushing us to prove them wrong. That's exactly what I did.

When I look back now, I'm amazed at how everything fell into place. It wasn't that it was easy – far from it – but the obstacles I had feared turned out to be surmountable once I found the right resources and support. My 'mushy' mind, as I called it back then, had made everything seem more complicated than it really was. I had convinced myself that college was out of reach, that it was too hard, too expensive, and too far beyond my grasp. But once I took that first step, everything else started to fall into place.

By the time I graduated, I felt a sense of accomplishment that went far beyond the diploma I held in my hand. I had proven to myself that I was capable of achieving my dreams, even when the odds weren't in my favor. I had learned to trust my instincts, to seek out opportunities, and to never underestimate my own resilience. Completing college wasn't just about getting a degree—it was about discovering what I was made of.

That experience shaped me in profound ways. It gave me the courage to pursue a career that would pay me more than just a high school diploma ever could, and it taught me that when I invest in myself, the returns are limitless. The education I received wasn't just about academics; it was about learning how to navigate the world on my own terms. And that, more than anything, is what gave me the confidence to keep moving forward, no matter what challenges came my way.

And they did. As I moved forward in my career, I took on roles that allowed me to provide for myself and build a secure future. However, as life often does, it soon presented me with new responsibilities—ones that required not only the skills I had developed in school and work but also the ability to balance my personal life with my professional ambitions.

Motherhood brought a new set of challenges. When my daughter was born, I was working as a loan officer. My job was commission-based, which meant that if I didn't work, I didn't get paid. I was terrified of losing my income, so just days after giving birth, I went back to work. I didn't allow myself the time to bond with my newborn, and I did the same thing after my son was born. It wasn't until years later that I realized the emotional toll it had taken—not just on me, but on my children. I was so focused on providing for them that I missed out on the moments that really mattered.

Looking back, I regret that decision. I didn't know at the time, but I had insurance that would cover my leave. If I had taken a moment to ask, to check, I could have stayed home with my babies without worrying about money. But I was so caught up in the fear of losing my income that I jumped right back into work, not realizing the cost it would have on my family. That was one of the hardest emotional hurdles to overcome—realizing that I had sacrificed time with my children because of fear. If I could go back, I would have done things differently. But I've made peace with that decision, and now I make up for it with my grandchildren. I take the time to be present with them, to savor every moment, knowing how quickly those early years pass by.

Forgiving myself for that mistake wasn't easy, but it was necessary. I carried the guilt with me for so long, feeling like I had let my children down. But I eventually realized that I did the best I could with the knowledge and resources I had at the time. Forgiving myself allowed me to move forward and become the mother and grandmother I wanted to be.

This journey of motherhood, career, and personal growth was one where I learned lessons from my past. Being the youngest of seven gave me the unique opportunity to learn from my older siblings' experiences. I saw their mistakes and successes, and I tried to avoid the pitfalls they encountered. I observed how they navigated relationships, career choices, and life's difficulties, and in many ways, I felt fortunate to have that knowledge to guide me.

One significant lesson I learned was about choosing the right person to share your life with. I had seen my siblings struggle in relationships where they weren't treated as equals, and I knew I didn't want that for myself. I didn't want a partner who would try to control every aspect of my life or dictate my choices. Instead, I wanted someone who would walk beside me, someone who would treat me as an equal. That understanding helped me navigate my own relationship with my husband. We've been together for over 36 years now, and while we've certainly had our challenges, the key to our longevity has been mutual respect and support. He's always been there for me, supporting the changes I've wanted to make, and while we've had our share of arguments—what relationship doesn't? —I've always felt comfortable knowing we are equals in this journey.

Of course, we argue. Words are exchanged, and sometimes, I regret the things I say in the heat of the moment. But, at the end of the day, it's the respect we hold for each other that keeps us going. I'm fortunate to have a partner who supports me, even when we don't always see eye to eye.

However, there were moments when I felt completely lost, unsure of what direction to take. But faith has always been a central part of my life, guiding me through both the good times and the bad. And in those moments, I leaned on my faith. I believed that God had a plan for me, even if I couldn't see it at the time. One experience stands out in my mind—when I was transitioning between jobs, unsure of what the future held. I had three children at home and knew I needed a job that allowed me to be more present with them.

One night, I had a vivid dream that felt so real it still lingers with me to this day. I found myself in the middle of a storm, the win howling fiercely around me as if it could tear me apart at my moment. Dark, rushing waters surged all around, the current relentless and wild. The waves crashed against me, their cold, merciless grip pulling me under. I struggled to stay afloat, gasping for air as I thrashed about, desperately searching for something to hold onto. My arms flailed in the darkness, trying to grasp a tree branch or any solid ground, but there was nothing. Just the powerful, swirling waters threatening to sweep me away.

The sky above was thick with storm clouds, black and oppressive, swirling like an angry vortex. Rain pelted down in sheets, soaking me to the bone and blurring my vision as I fought to keep my head above the surface. My heart raced, and fear tightened its grip around my chest. I had no idea where to turn; no direction seemed safe, and no escape appeared in sight.

Just when I thought the storm would swallow me whole, something changed. The dark clouds began to part, and a single beam of light broke through the chaos above. It was as if the heavens had opened up, and in that moment, everything seemed to pause. The roaring wind quieted, the raging waters stilled, and the rain softened to a gentle drizzle.

From that light, I heard a voice—a voice that was calm and reassuring, cutting through the storm with a sense of peace I hadn't felt in ages. It wasn't loud or commanding, but it was unmistakably powerful. The voice simply told me, "I am proud of you. Everything is going to be okay." And in that instant, all the fear and anxiety melted away. The storm that had felt so overwhelming no longer held power over me. Instead, I felt a profound sense of calm wash over me, as though the waters themselves had released their grip, and I was now being gently carried to safety.

MAMA'S PEARLS

When I woke from that dream, the feeling of peace stayed with me. It was more than just a dream—it was a message, a sign that I wasn't alone in this struggle, that there was a plan for me, even if I couldn't see it yet. That dream gave me the strength I needed to keep going, to trust that God had a plan for me and that I just needed to have faith.

Shortly after, an opportunity presented itself in the most unexpected way. I found a job at a call center just five minutes from my home—something that perfectly fit the needs of my family and myself. It wasn't the stormy struggle I had been expecting; instead, it was the calm after the storm, a place where I could work and still be present for my family. I stayed at that job for ten years, and it brought stability and peace to my life during the time when I needed it most.

When I reflect on who I've become today, I think my younger self would be in awe. There was a time when I was scared all the time, doubting whether I could handle what life threw at me. If I could go back and meet that young girl, I would give her a big hug and tell her she did well. I'd tell her that despite the fear and the doubt, she had the strength to push through. I think she'd be proud of me. She wouldn't have imagined the strength and resilience I've developed, but I'd remind her that it was inside her all along.

And while that younger version of me would marvel at the strength I've built, there are ways in which I've grown that others might not immediately see but are deeply meaningful to me. Life has a way of humbling you. When you experience enough, especially as a parent, you begin to see things differently. I used to look at other parents and judge them, criticizing the way they raised their children when things didn't go well. I thought to myself, "That would never happen with my kids." But life has a way of proving you wrong. As a mother, I've faced my own challenges, especially with my daughter, and I found myself in the same situations I had once judged others for.

It humbled me. It taught me that no one has all the answers, and we're all just doing the best we can. Having my own struggles with my children made me more accepting and forgiving, not only of others but of myself. I realized that the harsh judgment I once passed wasn't helpful—it was a reflection of my lack of understanding. Now, I'm more patient and compassionate, willing to help my children find their way back when they veer off course, rather than pushing them away or giving up on them. I learned not to follow the rigid approach of kicking someone out when they falter but to hold them close, helping them rebuild and get back on track.

That growth—learning to be more accepting, forgiving, and patient—has been one of the most profound changes in my life. It has humbled me in ways I never expected and made me a better person. And I think that's what life does. It doesn't just make you stronger—it teaches you compassion, humility, and understanding. And for that, I am deeply grateful.

MAMA'S PEARLS

SYLVIA VILLASENOR

My father wasn't just thinking about the present—he was thinking about the future, about the opportunities he wanted for his children, the better life he believed we could have in this new country. Love, in that moment, wasn't the warm, comforting kind; it was tough and painful. It required leaving behind the familiar for the unknown, sacrificing immediate comfort for long-term gain. That's the thing about love—it doesn't always feel good at the moment, but when you look back, you see how it was always working for your good. I see that now in the way my own children have benefitted from the choices my father made. Love is often forward-thinking, making decisions today for the benefit of tomorrow, even if it's hard at the moment.

Being a parent has taught me some of the hardest lessons about love. When your children are small, love feels simple and straightforward. They rely on you for everything, from their meals to their bedtime stories, and their love for you is complicated. You are their world, and everything you do seems to make sense to them. In those early years, its easy to feel like love is enough, that your relationship with them is based on this natural bond that requires little effort beyond caring for their needs.

But as they grow older, that bond shifts. Suddenly, love is no longer just about taking care of them; it's about guiding them, often in ways they don't appreciate at the time. It becomes more complex, especially when you have to set boundaries or say no. I remember so many moments when my children were upset with me, angry even because I had to make decisions they didn't agree with or understand. Whether it was about not allowing them to go somewhere, spend time with certain friends, or indulge in things I knew weren't good for them, I often found myself in the position of the "bad guy."

As a parent, you want to protect your children from the world from making mistakes that you know they will regret. But children don't see that when they're in the thick of it. To them, saying no feels like a punishment, an unfair limitation. And it's hard. It would have been easy to let my own frustration rise in response to their anger, to snap back when they were being disrespectful or demanding. But love doesn't work that way. Love teaches you patience, even when it's the hardest thing to muster. It teaches you to step back, to take a breath, and to remember why you're setting those boundaries in the first place.

I learned, over time, that love requires me to hold back my own emotions. There were so many instances where I wanted to just yell, to show them how frustrated I was that they couldn't see things my way. But deep down, I knew that wouldn't help. I had to let their anger cool, give them space, and wait for the right moment to explain my reasoning. There were times I had to remind myself that I was the adult in the situation, that I couldn't expect them to understand things the way I did because they simply didn't have the life experience. Love, in those moments, meant putting my own frustration aside and choosing to stay calm, to find the right words when they were ready to hear them.

SYLVIA VILLASENOR

And those words, the ones I waited for— "Mom, you were right"—they meant everything. Not because I needed the validation but because it was proof that love had done its job. It wasn't about being right; it was about knowing that the choices I made and the boundaries I set were in their best interest. My goal was never to control them or limit their experiences. It was to protect them, to help them navigate a world they couldn't fully understand yet. Love, in its truest form, is protective, but it's also patient. It's willing to wait for the right moment to reveal itself, to show that the tough decisions were made with the best intentions.

As a parent, you have to trust that what you're doing is enough, even when it feels like you're constantly hitting a wall. Love asks you to see the bigger picture, even when your children can't. It asks you to stay firm in your decisions, to know that one day, even if it's years down the road, they'll understand why you did what you did. And that's the humble part of being a parent. It's realizing that love isn't always about immediate results. It's about playing the long game, trusting that the seeds you plant today will grow into something meaningful in the future.

Looking back, one of the most unexpected ways love showed up in my life was through the process of finding the home where I still live today. At the time, it felt like anything but love. It was a period of frustration, stress, and a fair amount of anger. But now, as I reflect on that moment, I can see how love—and perhaps even divine guidance—was working behind the scenes, pushing me toward something better, something I didn't even know I needed.

MAMA'S PEARLS

The true story began when my sister Jeannie, who I had been renting a house from, came to me out of the blue and said she needed her house back. Jeannie had been living in the house she bought with her first husband; after their divorce, she was granted full ownership. When she remarried in 1988, she moved out to move in with her new husband and her children. I moved to her house in September of 1988 with my husband while I was eight months pregnant with Joy. Years passed and my two boys were also born while we lived in this house. My family and I had been renting it from her for ten years. It was comfortable, it was familiar, and I had no plans of moving to a new place right in the middle of the school year.

But life doesn't always follow the plans we make. Jeannie's second marriage was falling apart, and she needed to move back into her house, the house I was renting. She asked me to move out, and she wanted it done fast—far faster than I was prepared for. I had three young children, a live-in babysitter who helped me manage everything while I worked long hours, and two dogs. The thought of uprooting all of that and finding a new place to live seemed overwhelming.

I was caught off guard, frustrated, and, frankly, angry. I couldn't understand why she was putting this pressure on me, why she was tearing down the kitchen to start renovations before I had even found a new place to go. The timing couldn't have been worse, and I felt cornered. I remember feeling so helpless, unsure of how I was going to pull it all together in such a short amount of time. I didn't want to move into just any place; I needed a home, not just a temporary fix.

But it felt like Jeannie's needs were overshadowing mine, and there was little I could do about it.

Still, with no other choice, I began searching for a new house. It was during this time that something strange happened, something I couldn't see as a blessing at the moment. While I was looking, I came across a home in a neighborhood I hadn't considered before. It wasn't on my radar, and under normal circumstances, I don't think I would have even thought to look there. But when I found it, something clicked. It wasn't just a house; it felt right in a way I couldn't explain.

The home was owned by a woman who had multiple properties, and the real estate market had taken a downturn, making it difficult for her to manage all of them. She had two mortgages on this particular house, and the renters before me hadn't exactly been ideal tenants. The neighbors weren't fond of the wild parties that had been happening there, and she was eager to get a family in the home—someone who would care for the property and the neighborhood.

When I inquired about renting it, the process moved so fast that it made my head spin. The owner ran my credit, and everything checked out perfectly. She offered me a six-month lease with an option to buy, which was more than I had hoped for. I had never considered owning a home at that point, but it suddenly became a possibility. Not only that, but she even asked me to pick out new tile and make changes to the house, treating me like I was already the homeowner before I had even signed the lease.

MAMA'S PEARLS

We moved in with the kids and my babysitter, grateful to have found a place so quickly. And just 30 days after moving in, everything fell into place. The owner's loan officer contacted me, and I put in my loan application. To my surprise, the owner paid for everything— the appraisal and the closing costs. I didn't have to put a single penny down. In the span of one month, I went from being a renter, feeling stressed and overwhelmed by the sudden need to move, to becoming a homeowner. It was as if the universe had conspired to make this transition as smooth as possible, even though, at the time, it felt like anything but smooth.

That's when I realized something profound: this house, this new life I had stumbled into, was a gift. It was love in a form I hadn't recognized at first. It wasn't the soft, comforting love I was used to—it was love that pushed me out of my comfort zone, forced me to face uncertainty, and guided me to something better. If Jeannie hadn't needed her house back so suddenly, I might never have found this place. I might still have been living there, paying rent, and feeling secure, but not really moving forward.

But love, in its mysterious way, had other plans for me. It guided me to this home where my children grew up, where we created memories that would last a lifetime. And, perhaps most importantly, it showed me that sometimes the things we think are disruptions, the moments that feel unfair or overwhelming, are actually opportunities in disguise. They're love, working behind the scenes, pushing us toward what we truly need.

SYLVIA VILLASENOR

The grammar school my children attended was a half block from our new home. It was perfect—safe, close by, and exactly the kind of environment I wanted for them. Before, I had been sending my kids to a school that was several miles away, and my babysitter had to take the bus back and forth to drop and pick them up. Now, everything was within walking distance, and I didn't have to worry as much. I even began to think that this home was meant for us all along, that we were being guided here without even knowing it.

This house has been our home since 1999, and I'm still amazed at how it all came together. What began as a stressful, frustrating experience turned out to be one of the greatest blessings of my life. It's a reminder that love doesn't always show up the way we expect it to. Sometimes, it comes in the form of upheaval, of sudden changes that push us in directions we weren't planning to go. But in the end, love always guides us to where we're meant to be.

Over time, I've learned that love isn't always easy to recognize, and it's not always understood by others. There have been moments with my siblings when I tried to help, doing what I thought was an act of love, only to have my intentions misunderstood. It's a painful thing to feel like what you're offering from the heart is being taken the wrong way. But I've come to realize that love doesn't need validation to be real. It remains love, even when it isn't acknowledged or appreciated. You don't love for the sake of being thanked or understood. You love because it's what feels right because that's what love asks of you—to do what's good and true, even when it goes unrecognized.

MAMA'S PEARLS

Marriage has been another teacher in the art of love. Early on, I thought love was about happiness and fulfilling each other's expectations. But over the years, I learned that love is much more than that. It's about compromise. There were times when I was holding on to my own ideas too tightly, refusing to see things from my husband's perspective. But love, real love, doesn't demand its own way. It asks you to soften, to listen, to meet the other person halfway. There were nights when I'd laid in bed, replaying a disagreement in my head, realizing that maybe I wasn't entirely right. That's the humility that love brings – it teaches you to let go of your pride, to admit when you are wrong, and to grow together instead of growing apart.

And sometimes, you have to redefine love.

In relationships, both with my children and my spouse, I have had to learn when to let go and when to step back and allow them to make their own decisions, even when I didn't agree. Love isn't about control – it's about allowing others the space to grow, to make mistakes, and to find their own way. That's not easy, especially for someone like me who tends to want things a certain way. But love, real love, requires flexibility. It requires you to meet people where they are, not where you want them to be.

As I look back on all these moments, I see how love has shaped me, how it has guided me through some of the hardest decisions and some of the most beautiful ones. Love has been the constant, the thing that has held everything together, even when life felt like it was falling apart. It has asked me to give up things I thought I needed, only to show me that it's not about getting what you want – it's about giving, sacrificing, and being there for the people you care about, even when it is hard.

And that's the real power of love – it doesn't always make sense at the moment, but when you look back, you see that it was there all along, guiding you, shaping you, and leading you to exactly where you were meant to be.

And as it's rightly said,

"Love doesn't just sit there, like a stone; it has to be made, like bread, remade all the time, made new."

Ursula K. Le Guin.

MAMA'S PEARLS

SYLVIA VILLASENOR

Chapter 8
Strength in Adversity

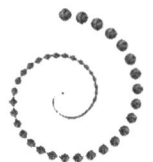

Strength is often built in the quiet moments – those times when you feel alone, when the weight of the world presses down on your shoulders, and when no one can truly understand what you are going through. In those moments, resilience becomes not just a choice but a lifeline. My life has been full of such moments, instances where strength and resilience were crucial. And it is through these experiences that I have come to understand that strength isn't the absence of struggle but rather the ability to rise in the face of it.

One of the most significant challenges in my life was balancing the demands of my career with the needs of my family. As a working mother, there were many days when I felt torn between two worlds – my responsibilities at work and my desire to be there for my children. For over 14 years, our babysitter, Maria, played a pivotal role in our lives. She became a second mother to my kids, always there when I couldn't be.

MAMA'S PEARLS

There were moments when the guilt was overwhelming. I would come home from a long day at work, exhausted and ready to connect with my children, but the house would already be quiet. I would see them sitting with Maria, their faces full of excitement as they recounted the events of their day. Their stories, their triumphs, their struggles – all of it had already been shared. By the time they turned to me, it felt like there was nothing left. I would ask, "How was your day?" And they would respond with a short, "It was fine, Mom," before retreating back into whatever they were doing.

I would sit at the dinner table, watching them laugh with Maria, the woman who had become their confidante, their constant companion, while I was the one working to provide for them. The distance between us, though not intentional, grew wider with every passing day. It wasn't just the big things I was missing, like school plays or birthday parties—it was the small, everyday moments that cut the deepest. The hugs after a bad day, the first time they learned something new, or even the silly little jokes that bonded us. These were the moments that made up their childhood, and I wasn't there to experience them.

I remember thinking, *Is this how it's going to be? Will they always turn to her instead of me?* That thought would haunt me during the quiet moments at work when I would catch myself staring at a family photo on my desk, wondering if I was doing the right thing. Was my ambition, my need to provide a better life for them, actually pushing them further away? I couldn't help but question myself, feeling like I was stuck in an impossible situation where, no matter what I did, I was losing something precious.

The guilt wasn't just emotional—it was physical. It weighed on me like a heavy blanket, following me everywhere I went. It was in the quick dinners, the late-night work emails, but my husband and I never missed parent-teacher conferences. Each time I rushed out of the door in the morning or came home late, I felt like I was choosing my career over my children. And even though I knew deep down that I was working for them to give them a better future, it didn't stop the pangs of guilt that gnawed at me.

It wasn't just about missing out on their lives; it was about the fear of losing that special connection only a mother can have with her children. I wondered if they saw me as a stranger in their own home, someone who was there but not really present. There were nights when I would lie awake, thinking about how things could have been different. If I had worked less, if I had made more time for them, would they have confided in me instead? Would they have run to me with their problems, their dreams, their questions about life?

It was a constant battle between my desire to be a good mother and my need to be successful in my career. I wanted to have it all, but there were times when it felt like I was failing at both. I wasn't the mom who could pick her kids up from school every day or help them with their homework in the afternoons. Instead, I was the mom who showed up late after the day already unfolded, hoping there was still something left for me to grasp onto.

MAMA'S PEARLS

The hardest part wasn't just the guilt – it was the fear that one day, my children wouldn't need me anymore. That they would have outgrown their need for my presence, for support, because they had already learned to rely on someone else. I feared becoming the outsider in their lives, the one who was always playing catch-up but never quite there in time. And that, more than anything, broke my heart.

But as difficult as those moments were, I knew I couldn't hold resentment. The babysitter was not only helping to raise my children, but she was also supporting me in ways I didn't fully appreciate at the time. She never spoke ill of me in front of my children, and she always made sure they understood that I was working hard for them, even if I was physically present. That kind of loyalty and support is rare, and looking back, I realize how fortunate I was to have her in our lives.

When Maria left, my son Dean was 14, and for the first time, I had more opportunities to be with my children. It wasn't easy at first – I had to rebuild the bond that had been somewhat weakened by my absence – but the time we spent together became more precious. I realized that my children understood far more than I gave them credit for. They knew I was working for them, and in the end, that made our bond stronger.

Another source of strength in my life came from my father. He was a strict man, especially with his daughters. Growing up, he imposed rules and limits that, at the time, felt suffocating. But as I have gotten older, I have come to understand that his strictness was his way of protecting us. He wanted to make sure we didn't make the mistakes he had seen others make. He wanted to keep us from falling into the traps of drugs, alcohol, or bad relationships.

In those days, my father's word was law. He ruled our home with a firm hand, his presence casting a long shadow over every decision we made. There were strict rules that we lived by, and questioning them was not an option. He watched over us like a hawk, always aware of where we were, who we were with, and what we were doing. It seemed like he had an instinct, an unspoken sense of when we were about to step out of line, and he would quickly intervene before we had the chance to make a mistake.

At the time, it felt like a prison. While other kids were enjoying their freedom—going to school dances, staying out late, and experimenting with things that were off-limits to us—we were held to a different standard. There were many things we simply weren't allowed to do. Sleepovers were rare, parties even rarer, and dating was completely out of the question until we were much older. As a teenager, I resented him for it. I couldn't understand why he was so strict, why he didn't trust us to make our own choices. It felt suffocating, like no matter what we did, we were always under his watchful eye.

But now, with the benefit of time and perspective, I realize that it wasn't about control or distrust—it was about protection. My father didn't want us to be like the kids he saw at school dances or in the neighborhood who were making choices that could ruin their lives. He saw the dangers we couldn't see—the lure of alcohol, drugs, bad relationships—and he was determined to keep us safe from those temptations. He knew that one wrong choice could set us on a path that would be difficult to return from, and as much as it frustrated me at the time, I now understand that his strictness came from a place of love.

He wanted to shield us from the mistakes that he had seen others make, from the hardships he had experienced or witnessed in his own life. In his mind, the world outside our home was filled with traps waiting to ensnare us, and he believed it was his duty as our father to keep us on the right path. He didn't want us to be influenced by peers who were experimenting with dangerous behaviors or drifting into lifestyles that could derail our futures.

Looking back, I can see the wisdom in his approach. At the time, we didn't understand the gravity of the choices being made by the kids around us. We saw freedom as something to be desired, not realizing that with it came risks we weren't mature enough to handle. My father saw the bigger picture—he saw the consequences that we couldn't see. He wasn't trying to deprive us of fun or independence; he was trying to give us the best chance at a good life. And now, as an adult, I realize how much effort that took on his part. It must have been exhausting, constantly keeping track of our whereabouts, setting boundaries, and reinforcing them with unwavering consistency. But he did it, day in and day out, because he believed it was the only way to keep us safe.

And while we didn't always appreciate it at the time, his guidance helped us avoid many of the pitfalls that others fell into. For that, I am deeply thankful. This kind of upbringing instilled in me a sense of resilience. I learned early on that life isn't always fair and that sometimes, the people who love you the most will push you the hardest. But in the end, it's for your own good. My father's demands, though tough, shaped the woman I would become. They taught me to be strong, to stand up for myself, and to make the right choices, even when it was difficult.

Life has a way of throwing curveballs when you least expect them. One such moment came when the call center where I worked as a mortgage loan originator for 10 years shut down. At the time, it felt like the end of the world. I had built a family of coworkers, and suddenly, that was taken away from me. I remember thinking, "What am I going to do now?" The uncertainty was overwhelming, and for the first time in a long time, I felt truly lost.

But as with most challenges in life, this one came with an unexpected blessing. I found a new job at Bank of America, working as a mortgage loan officer. At first, I was terrified. I hadn't worked face-to-face with clients in years, and the thought of starting over in a new role was daunting. But I took the leap, and what I found was a job that not only suited me but also gave me more flexibility and fulfilment than I ever imagined.

Working with clients, especially in a bilingual environment, was deeply rewarding. Many of the people I helped had been saving for years, unsure if they would ever qualify for a home loan. Being able to guide them through the process and help them achieve their dreams was incredibly satisfying. It reminded me that sometimes, the things we fear the most turn out to be the very things that bring us the greatest joy.

Looking back, I realize that the shutdown of the call center, as devastating as it seemed at the time, was a blessing in disguise. It forced me to step out of my comfort zone and embrace a new chapter in my life. And in doing so, I discovered strengths I didn't know I had.

Through all of life's challenges, one thing that has always sustained me is my faith. There were many times when I didn't know how I was going to make it through—times when the weight of adversity felt too heavy to bear. In those moments, I turned to prayer. I asked for guidance, for strength, and for the ability to see the light at the end of the tunnel, even when everything around me seemed dark.

Prayer became my anchor during the toughest times. It wasn't always easy to find the time or the focus to sit down and pray, especially when I was in the middle of a storm. But I've learned that resilience doesn't mean facing everything alone. It means knowing when to ask for help, whether that's from God, from family, or from friends.

There were moments when I couldn't see a way out, and the struggles felt insurmountable. But each time, something would shift. A door would open, an opportunity would present itself, or simply, the weight would lift, and I would find the strength to keep going. I believe that's the power of faith—knowing that even when you can't see the way, there's a higher power guiding you.

SYLVIA VILLASENOR

Adversity has a way of testing relationships. Over the years, I've faced challenges that have strained my relationships with those closest to me—my husband, my siblings, and even my children. When someone you love hurts you, it cuts deep. You wonder how they could say or do the things they did, and it's easy to hold onto resentment.

But one of the most important lessons I've learned is that forgiveness is a form of strength. Holding a grudge only weighs you down, while forgiveness allows you to move forward. It's not always easy, and there have been times when I've had to step away, give myself space to heal, and then come back when I was ready.

There were moments when I felt betrayed when the actions of those closest to me hurt more than I thought possible. But I knew that cutting them off wasn't an option. Family is family, and no matter how difficult things get, you find a way to make it work. It takes strength to forgive, to move past the hurt, and to rebuild those relationships.

As I reflect on the challenges I've faced, I realize that resilience is not just something you develop for yourself—it's something you pass on to others. Whether it's through the example you set for your children, the support you offer to friends, or the wisdom you share with younger generations, resilience becomes a legacy.

For me, that legacy comes from my mother, from my father, and from the many people who have supported me along the way. It's the knowledge that no matter what life throws at you, you have the strength to rise. And it's my hope that through my story, readers will find the strength within themselves to face their own challenges, to rise above their own adversities, and to build a legacy of resilience for those who come after them.

Life is a stormy sea, unpredictable and relentless, with waves that can toss you from side to side, making it hard to stay on course. Sometimes, the tide pulls you under, and for a moment, it feels as though you'll never resurface. But resilience, like the anchor of a ship, keeps you steady even when the waters are rough. It's that invisible strength deep within that keeps you from drifting away, no matter how hard the winds blow. It's the ability to stand firm in the face of adversity, even when every fiber of your being wants to give in.

As I reflect on my journey, I've come to realize that life isn't about avoiding the storms—it's about learning how to sail through them. There were times when I faced hardships that felt insurmountable. Days when the weight of responsibility felt like a heavy stone tied to my chest, dragging me down into the depths of guilt and doubt. But through those moments, I discovered something powerful: strength isn't always loud. It doesn't always roar like thunder. Sometimes, it's quiet. It's the whisper in the back of your mind that says, *Keep going, even when you don't know how.*

Strength is often like a tree rooted deep in the earth. On the surface, it sways with the wind, bending under the pressure of life's challenges. But beneath the ground, its roots are strong and unmoving, stretching deep into the soil, holding it firm against the forces trying to uproot it. In the same way, resilience is what keeps us grounded, even when life threatens to knock us over.

One of the greatest lessons I've learned is that failure, disappointment, and hardship are not dead ends—they are crossroads. When one door closes, it might feel like the end of a journey, but in truth, it's the start of a new path. It's like walking through a forest and finding that the trail you've been following suddenly disappears. At first, you panic, unsure of where to go next. But as you look around, you realize there are many other paths winding through the trees, waiting to be explored.

Sometimes, the doors we want to open are the very ones that lead us astray. We push and push, desperate to force our way through, but there is wisdom in the doors that remain closed. It's life's way of protecting us from paths not meant for us. Like a wise gatekeeper, it knows when to guide us elsewhere, even when we're too focused on what we think we want. I've learned that there's strength in accepting when a door isn't meant to open and resilience in trusting that another opportunity is waiting just around the corner.

And when the right door does open, even if it feels unfamiliar or intimidating, that's when you step forward, even if your heart is full of fear. Strength is not the absence of fear—it's walking forward in spite of it. It's like standing on the edge of a cliff, knowing you have to jump, even though you can't see the bottom. You leap, not because you're unafraid but because you trust that the wings you've been given will carry you through the unknown.

Resilience isn't just about surviving hardships—it's about thriving in the face of them. It's about seeing adversity not as a roadblock but as a stepping stone to something greater. Like a blacksmith forges iron in fire, life's challenges shape us, refining our spirits and making us stronger than we ever thought we could be.

I want readers to understand that when they face life's storms, it's okay to feel overwhelmed. It's okay to feel lost, scared, or even angry. But know this: within you is a strength that can weather any storm. Sometimes, it's not about fighting the wind but about bending with it, letting it pass, and rising again once the storm has moved on. Strength is like a candle flickering in the darkness. It may waver, but it never goes out. And in those moments of darkness, when it feels like the light is fading, that's when resilience steps in and keeps the flame alive.

The hardest part of life's journey is often letting go—letting go of what you thought you wanted, of the path you thought you'd follow, or the outcome you thought was guaranteed. It's like holding onto a rope that's slipping through your fingers, and every instinct tells you to hold on tighter. But true strength is in knowing when to let go and trusting that the fall won't break you. In fact, it might be what sets you free.

At the heart of this message is the idea that resilience is a choice. It's a mindset, a decision to keep moving forward, even when everything inside you wants to stop. And the beauty of resilience is that it grows stronger with each challenge. Just like a muscle that becomes more powerful through repeated use, our ability to withstand life's difficulties increases every time we face adversity and rise again.

So, when life knocks you down – and it will, because it knocks us all down at some point – remember this: you have the strength to get back up. Like a seed buried deep in the soil, you might feel like you are covered in darkness, but that's where growth happens. Slowly, steadily, you will push through the dirt and reach toward the light, stronger and more resilient than before.

Trust the process. Trust yourself. And trust that even when the road ahead looks uncertain, you have within you everything you need to navigate it. Strength is not just about holding on—it's about knowing when to let go, when to trust, and when to embrace the new opportunities life places before you.

MAMA'S PEARLS

Chapter 9
Passing on the Pearls

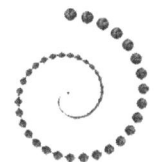

As I sit here reflecting on the years that have passed, one lesson stands out more than any other: we are not meant to walk this journey of life alone. Just as my mother left behind her pearls of wisdom for us to carry forward, it is now my responsibility – and the responsibility of every one of us – to pass on those lessons to the next generation. There is a simple yet profound beauty in the act of sharing what we have learned, the things that have shaped us, the moments that have tested our spirit, and the choices that led us to where we are today.

Passing on these pearls of wisdom isn't just a gift to others – it's a way to continue the legacy of those who came before us. My mother's strength, resilience, and unwavering love were her gifts to us, and though her time with us was far too short, the values she imparted remain as vivid today as they were all those years ago. The simple things she taught us—respect for elders, the power of perseverance, and the importance of keeping an open heart—have guided me through the darkest and brightest moments of my life. These pearls of wisdom have been passed down, and now it is my turn and yours to keep that tradition alive.

Over the years, I have had many conversations with my children, friends, and younger colleagues who sought guidance, and it became clear to me how important it is to listen, understand, and offer what we can from our own experiences.

One memory that stands out took place when I worked with a group of young women much younger than me. Despite the age difference, we bonded over our shared experiences. We sat together in the lunchroom, and many of them would confide in me, asking how I managed to balance my life and how I navigated the complexities of relationships and work. These were women in their twenties, just starting their own journeys, while I was in my late forties. Despite the generation gap, our conversations transcended age. They saw me not just as an older colleague but as someone who had lived through what they were going through.

Many of the young women were struggling to balance personal dreams with societal expectations. One recurring theme in our conversations was their desire to succeed both in their relationships and their careers. They were navigating the same crossroads I had faced decades earlier—the choice between being a stay-at-home mom or continuing their career paths. I was happy to share my experiences with them because I had once been in their shoes. I had to make similar decisions, and I knew how daunting it could be.

SYLVIA VILLASENOR

One young woman, Veronica, confided in me about her husband. He had not yet immigrated, and she was in the process of fixing his papers. At that time, he had to return to his home country for nine months, leaving her alone with their new baby. The strain was palpable, and Veronica often seemed overwhelmed, but I could tell she was doing her best to stay strong. We sat down for countless conversations, and she shared her worries about being apart from him for so long and the challenges of raising their baby alone.

I told her about my own family's experiences with immigration and separation. I had seen similar situations many times as a child, watching family members go through the same struggles. I reminded her that nine months, although difficult, was a standard process and that, eventually, the time would pass. *"Stay strong, stay focused, and remember that this is temporary,"* I told her. *"Soon enough, you'll be together, and this hard chapter will be behind you."* Veronica appreciated those talks, and I could see the relief in her eyes when I reassured her that everything would be okay. She later asked me for a recommendation letter for her husband's paperwork, which I gladly provided, knowing how important this was for her family.

Sometime later, after I had moved on from that job, Veronica called me. She told me that her husband was finally back, and everything had worked out just as I had said it would. It was a moment that reminded me of how meaningful it is to offer guidance and encouragement when others are going through their most difficult times. Sometimes, all we need is someone who has been through it before to tell us that we can get through it, too.

Always listen to understand, not just with our ears but with our hearts. The stories and experiences of those who have walked the path before us are invaluable. So often, we think that our struggles are unique and that no one can understand what we are going through. But the truth is, many have been in our shoes, facing the same mountains to climb, and their insights can shine a light on the path ahead.

I think back to conversations with my father; his voice tinged with the weariness of someone who had faced more battles than he cared to recount. I didn't always understand the depth of his words at the time, but looking back, I see how much wisdom he was trying to impart.

"Be patient," he would say. *"Life doesn't always go as planned, but if you keep moving forward, it will take you where you are meant to be."*

There were his pearls, passed to me through quiet moments of reflection and through his actions more than his words. As a child, I didn't always appreciate what he was saying. But as I grew, I learned to value his perspective to seek out the knowledge of those who had lived through their own trials.

The experiences of our elders are not just stories to be heard and forgotten. They are lessons and treasures that can guide us through our own lives. When my daughter was younger, she would sometimes ask me for advice about things she was going through.

SYLVIA VILLASENOR

"What would you do, Mom?" she would ask. I would tell her what I had done when I faced similar situations and whether it had worked out or not. Sometimes, she followed my advice, and other times, she didn't. But the fact that she asked showed me that she valued the experiences I had lived through.

There was a time when she sat across from me, her face marked by uncertainty. She was in her 30s, at that pivotal moment in life when you've started to shape your path but still question if you're going the right way. *"What should I do, Mom?"* she asked. I could see in her eyes the same mix of hope and doubt that I had carried at her age.

I told her, the wisdom passed down through generations. *"It's not always about what you think is the fastest route. Sometimes, you just have to trust the process. Don't be afraid to make mistakes. Whatever decision you make, you'll learn from it."* She listened intently, nodding, though I knew she would still wrestle with her choices, as we all do.

Sometimes, my advice resonated with her, and she followed it, finding success or peace. Other times, she chose a different path, learning her own lessons along the way. And I'm proud of her for that. Because that's what life is—a journey of decisions, of learning when to listen and when to trust yourself. The pearls of wisdom are there to guide you, but it's up to each person to decide how to apply them.

Then there's my son, Steven. He, too, came to me during a tough time. He was shifting careers, unsure if his next step was the right one. *"Mom, I've got an opportunity, but I don't know if it's what I really want to do,"* he admitted one evening. I could tell he was grappling with a decision that felt like it could change everything.

"Steven," I said, *"opportunities don't always look like we expect them to. Keep your mind open. Even if this isn't exactly what you planned, it might lead you somewhere better. You don't have to have it all figured out right now."* I watched as his face softened with relief. Sometimes, all we need is to hear that it's okay not to have all the answers. He went on to take that job, and while it wasn't the career-defining moment he thought it might be, it opened doors to future opportunities he hadn't foreseen.

It's in these moments with my children that I realize how important it is to pass on what we've learned. But passing on wisdom isn't just about telling someone what to do—it's about being there, listening, and allowing them to find their own way, with the benefit of your experience to guide them. My children may not always take my advice, but they always know that I'm here for them, ready to offer the pearls I've gathered throughout my life whenever they're ready to receive them.

That's what passing on the pearls is all about. It's about sharing what you've learned, whether from triumph or failure and offering it as a gift to those who are coming up behind you. They may not always take your advice, and that's okay. But the act of sharing—of being open and vulnerable with your experiences—creates a bridge between generations.

SYLVIA VILLASENOR

Words are important, but actions speak louder. This is something, not through lectures but through the way she lived her life. She didn't just tell us to be strong; she showed us what strength looked like. She didn't just talk about love; she lived it, even when it was hard. And in doing so, she passed on the most important pearls of all.

One of the greatest challenges of passing on wisdom is realizing that it's not about forcing someone to learn. It's about leading by example. When we live with integrity, when we embody the lessons we've learned, we become walking testaments to those around us.

As we grow older, we gain something more than just experience – we gain the responsibility to share that experience with others. It's easy to think that younger generations may not want to hear what we have to say. They may seem too busy, too preoccupied with their own lives to care about the lessons we have learned. But this is precisely why it's so important to pass on what we know. We don't share our wisdom because we think we have all the answers; we share it because we have been where they are now.

I have seen this with my own children and grandchildren. Sometimes, they listen intently to my stories and advice, eager to absorb the lessons I have learned over the years. I can see the way they lean in, their eyes soft with understanding, as if they are carefully tucking my words away for future use. Those moments feel rewarding, as though the wisdom I've collected throughout my life has found its next home. But there are also times when my advice seems to fall on deaf ears, when they brush it off with a confident smile, believing they already know best. It's in these moments I see the younger version of myself in them—headstrong, certain that I could figure it out on my own, even when the guidance of those who came before me was right there, ready to be offered.

And that's okay. I've come to realize that not every lesson can be learned by simply hearing it. Some lessons need to be lived and experienced firsthand, with all the bumps and bruises that come along the way. Life has a way of teaching us, even when we think we already have the answers. My children and grandchildren are no different from me in that regard. There were countless times my own people offered me guidance, and I smiled politely, thinking to myself, *"I'll do it my way."* Only later, when I faced the consequences of my choices, did I understand the value of what they had tried to tell me.

I've learned to be patient to accept that some pearls need time to sink in. Wisdom doesn't always reveal its worth immediately. Sometimes, it takes years before we truly understand the meaning behind the advice we were given. When my children or grandchildren choose a different path from the one I suggested, I don't feel frustrated anymore. I trust that they are walking the road they need to walk and that, in time, they'll reflect on our conversations with a newfound appreciation for what I was trying to convey.

There's a certain humility that comes with watching your loved ones make their own way. It's a reminder that no matter how much we want to protect them, to shield them from the mistakes we've made, they, too, need to stumble a little, to fall, to get back up and learn on their own terms. Those are the moments when the pearls of wisdom we've shared, seemingly ignored at first, suddenly become relevant. It's in the aftermath of their own trials and tribulations that they start to see the value of the lessons I've passed down.

As parents and grandparents, we sometimes want to wrap our loved ones in a bubble of protection to steer them away from pain and hardship. But that's not how life works. Some lessons simply can't be taught by words alone – they must be lived. And they are that's when our advice comes back to them. That's when they begin to appreciate the value of those pearls we have been offering all along.

It's a cycle I've come to accept. The younger generation needs the space to explore, to make their own choices, and yes, even to make their own mistakes. But they also need to know that we're here for them, always, with open arms and a wellspring of understanding. In time, they'll come back, not just for more advice, but for the comfort of knowing that someone has walked this path before them.

I've seen it happen again and again. My grandchildren, as young and vibrant as they are, sometimes brush off my stories with a smile that says, "I've got this, Grandma." I smile back, knowing full well that one day, they'll look back on our conversations with a different perspective. When they face their own challenges—perhaps a difficult relationship, a career setback, or the struggles of balancing work and family—they'll remember the things I've said. Maybe it won't happen right away, but eventually, those pearls will surface.

MAMA'S PEARLS

They'll realize that the advice I gave wasn't meant to dictate their choices but to offer them a foundation, a guiding light when things get tough.

And I'll be here, ready to share more, knowing that wisdom is not always a one-time gift. It's something that grows with them, alongside their experiences, and it blossoms when they're ready to receive it. It's in those moments when they circle back to me for guidance after they've lived through their own experiences that I know the pearls of wisdom I've passed on have truly found their place.

Each conversation, each moment of guidance, is like planting a seed. It may not take root right away, but eventually, it will grow.

In the end, this chapter of life is about more than just sharing what we know. It is about recognizing that we are part of something much bigger than ourselves. The pearls we pass on today will shape the future, just as the pearls we received have shaped our lives. And in that way, we are all connected—past, present, and future.

So, I urge you, dear reader, to pass on your own pearls of wisdom. Share what you have learned, not only with your family but with anyone who may benefit from your experience. You never know who you may touch and whose life you may change by simply offering the gift of your knowledge, your strength, and your love.

Conclusion

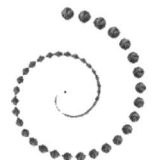

As I sit here reflecting on this journey of writing, I realize how deeply it has taken me back through my own life, uncovering lessons and emotions I hadn't revisited in years. These conversations have drawn out memories I thought I'd long since moved past, and in doing so, they've reminded me of one undeniable truth: everything I've gone through, all the good and bad, had a purpose. There were times I could have made better choices and times when my own missteps made the path harder than it needed to be. But as I look back now, I wouldn't be so hard on myself. Those mistakes, those struggles—they shaped who I am today.

If I could offer one final piece of advice to those who find themselves struggling, it would be this: don't let your mistakes define you. Forgive yourself sooner because life is too short to be spent in regret. I spent far too long being hard on myself, and I wish I had found the strength earlier to forgive my mistakes. If I had, I would have had the confidence to keep moving forward instead of stalling.

MAMA'S PEARLS

Life has a way of knocking you down sometimes. It can feel like you're being hit from all directions, like a punching bag with no end in sight. You shrink into yourself, unsure of where to turn or how to find the strength to keep going. During these times, it's easy to feel unworthy of love, to feel like you're not enough. But that's exactly when you need to dig deep and find that inner strength. For me, prayer has always been an important part of that process. Not in a religious sense but in a deeply personal, one-on-one connection with God. It's about having a relationship, the kind of relationship where you know you're accepted no matter what mistakes you've made.

As I look back, I often think about my mother's final days. She must have been so scared, knowing that she was leaving us behind. I can only imagine what was going through her mind as she lay in that hospital bed, knowing her time was short. We were her pearls, her most precious treasures, and she had to trust that we would be okay without her. That's the essence of this book—those pearls of wisdom she left behind and how they've shaped the lives of her children and grandchildren. Her legacy and my own are not just in the words we've spoken but in the lives we've touched along the way.

This book is my way of leaving something behind, a map for my children and their children to follow. It's a testament to the values my parents and grandparents instilled in me and how those values have shaped our family across generations. Even though my children and grandchildren grew up in a different environment from the one I did, these family values have stayed with us. I believe they will be passed down, talked about, and shared with future generations long after I'm gone.

In the end, this book is not for everyone. It's for those who might find healing in its pages, for those who are struggling, who need to know they are not alone. Pain can be overwhelming, but it can be lightened when we share it with someone who understands. And in the same way, happiness grows the more we spread it. Writing this book has been a way of sharing both—the pain and the joy—so that others might find comfort and strength in its pages.

This is my legacy. These are my pearls. And I hope, as you turn the final page, that you carry a little piece of this wisdom with you into your own life.

www.ingramcontent.com/pod-product-compliance
Lightning Source LLC
Chambersburg PA
CBHW051153120626
46547CB00012B/1061